ROCKET SCIENTISTS' GUIDE™ TO SPIRITUAL DISCERNMENT

I wish for the truth and nothing but the truth,
no compromise and no strings attached.

ROCKET SCIENTISTS'
GUIDE™ TO SPIRITUAL DISCERNMENT

By

Dr. Michael Sharp
www.michaelsharp.org

The Lightning Path
www.thelightningpath.com

Published by Lightning Path Press
St Albert, Alberta. Canada.
press.thelightningpath.com

Print ISBN 978-1-897455-16-6
Ebook ISBN 978-1-897455-17-3

Library and Archives Canada Cataloguing in Publication

Sharp, Michael, 1963-, author
 Rocket scientists' guide to spiritual discernment / by Dr. Michael Sharp.

Issued in print and electronic formats.
ISBN 978-1-897455-16-6 (paperback).--ISBN 978-1-897455-17-3 (epub)

 1. Religious leaders. 2. Spiritual life. I. Title.

BL626.38.S53 2015 206'.1 C2015-904106-6
C2015-904107-4

Table of Contents

Acknowledgments

I would like to thank Janet and Gerald Finnegan for their advice, suggestions, and editing expertise on this and several other books. Their contributions make this a powerful contribution to the practice of discernment.

I would like to thank Benjamin Pritchard for helpful, insightful, and useful discussions and dialogues on Lightning Path materials.

Finally, I would like to thank my wife and kids for just being there for me.

Preface

This is a book on spiritual discernment. This is a book designed to help you tell the difference between spiritual information likely to lead you towards authentic spiritual connection with higher consciousness (e.g. God, Brahman, Allah) and spiritual information likely to confuse you, spin you around in circles, and leave you spiritually impotent and disconnected.

From a certain point of view, this book is a basic spiritual text. This book deals with a basic problem that we all face which is winnowing the spiritual wheat from the useless and unproductive chaff. It is the kind of book that you should read at the start of your spiritual journey, because reading it can save time, energy, and possibly a little heartbreak. At another level, however, the book is not so basic. This book is built upon the basic and intermediate spiritual concepts of the Lightning Path (LP), in particular concepts provided in LP Workbook One through LP Workbook Three.[1]

---

[1] Michael Sharp, Lightning Path Workbook Three - Foundations, Lightning Path Workbook Series, ed. Michael Sharp, vol. 3 (St. Albert, Alberta: Lightning Path Press, 2017), Michael Sharp, Lightning Path Workbook One - Introduction to Authentic Spirituality, Lightning Path Workbook Series, vol. 1 (St. Albert, Alberta: Lightning Path Press, 2016), Michael Sharp, Lightning Path Workbook Two - Introduction to the Lightning Path, Lightning Path Workbook Series, St. Albert, Alberta..

Some of these concepts are novel to the LP and some are redefinitions. In all cases, when LP concepts are introduced they are highlighted in bold to draw your attention to them, defined in the main text or the footnote, and linked to the SpiritWiki for those wanting to explore a little deeper. If you find you are having difficulty wrapping your head around some of the ideas, concepts, and vocabulary in this book even with the definitions provided here, I encourage you to visit the Lightning Path site at http://www.thelightningpath.com/. There you will find the introductory LP texts conveniently available for download.

Parable of the Ships

Imagine for a moment the vast blue ocean, clear, crystal, and calm. Imagine yourself standing on a lookout, basking in the warm ocean breeze, and gazing out upon this ocean of vast stillness. Breathing deeply, you are calm and serene as you watch the waves roll across the glass surface.

For a time, you gaze, watching, breathing, but then you see a speck on the horizon. You breathe deeply, excited by the vision, and watch as the speck rolls its way towards you. It comes from a long distance and draws towards you leisurely. You squint at it wondering what it is. Soon enough the outline becomes clear and you see that it is an ocean liner, a passenger ship, steaming towards you. It continues to approach and as it does, you see it is not just any passenger ship. Even from a distance, you sense its magnificence. The curve of the hull, the silhouette of the multiple smoke stacks, the size and the grandeur mark it as the reigning monarch of modern cruise ships.

Standing on the deck, soaking in the breeze, you watch it approach in great anticipation and with growing excitement, but as it gets close your anticipation and excitement turns to shock and disbelief. As it gets close, you can see there is something horribly wrong. Up close, you can see that this ship is far from magnificent. Up close you can see it is decrepit, rusted, run down, banged up, crusted with gunk, dilapidated, and rusted so bad that holes are appearing in the hull. As you gaze at the ship in horror you think to yourself, "It is so bad that it must surely be in danger of sinking." and sure enough, as your eyes dart to the water line you notice the ship is going down.

It is at this point that the original anticipation and excitement totally evaporates and fear overtakes you. With a feeling of grave danger you wonder, "Are there any people on that ship?" You gaze at the deck and sure enough, people are standing, chatting, and milling about.

Your heart skips a beat. You wonder to yourself, how are they handling their sinking ship? What are they doing to avert disaster? You focus on their faces and become confused. "My God," you exclaim, "they don't know their ship is sinking". "Look at them", you cry, "they are smiling, laughing, eating, and drinking".

Slowly you realize, they are having a party.

Your eyes widen in horror.

"This can't be true," you cry.

"Can they not see their ship is sinking?"

"Do they not care they will drown in the ocean?"

You squint at the deck, looking for some explanation and then your heart quakes with fear.

There are children on the deck, and lots of them.

"Oh my god," you say as your consciousness leaps ahead to the time when the ship sinks and the children drown.

The thought of it brings tears to your eyes.

You cough and choke.

You brace yourself for the end, but just as despair threatens to overwhelm you, you notice another ship following not far behind.

You take a deep breath.

"Could it be?" you say.

"Is there hope?"

You turn your gaze to the new ship. At first, and from a distance, it looks much like the old ship. For a moment, you die inside thinking about the possibility of another disaster; but then, as it approaches, you see it is not like the first ship at all. Unlike the first ship, this ship is not run down and dilapidated. On the contrary, this one looks brand new, just out of the docks. It is shiny, bedazzling, and glorious with brilliant and elaborate gold trim.

What a wondrous sight it is, and lucky for those on board. As you think this, your gaze travels to the decks of the new ship where you expect to see people laughing and enjoying themselves, but to your surprise you find no one.

You peer into the portholes.

You scan down the hallways.

You wonder, who is steering the ship?

Your eyes scan forward looking for the bridge of the new ship and when you find it, you peer inside and sure enough, there's a helmsman, a captain, and a few others; but besides this small crew, there appears to be nobody else on the ship.

"Curious, but fortunate," you think as the fear begins to evaporate from your body. Here is another ship that is big enough to accommodate all the passengers of the old ship in splendor and luxury. What is even better, the captain of the new ship seems fully apprised of the situation. As you peer into the bridge, you can see he is gesticulating wildly, pointing at the old ship in front of him, and giving orders to those around him.

A feeling of relief floods through your body.

You watch as the gesticulating captain bolts out of the bridge and down onto the deck below. You notice he carries a megaphone in one hand, and a flare gun in the other. He runs forward to the tip of his ship, waits until his vessel is as close as possible, and then begins firing his flare gun to notify the revelers but oddly, they don't seem to notice. Instead, and despite their sinking ship, the revelers continue to party.

The captain looks confused.

He becomes more agitated.

Don't they see their ship is sinking, he thinks to himself.

Are they unaware of the danger?

Do they not care about the children?

Not giving up, he keeps firing his flares and shouting through his megaphone until finally a few individuals standing in the stern of the old ship look up and see him jumping up and down, gesticulating, and pointing down at the hull of their ship.

They are surprised to see another ship so close, but they are pleased to see it. They wave in greeting and watch the captain jump around. Not understanding why the captain is so agitated, and wanting to get back to their party, most of them smile, wave, and turn back to the party right away. But, a couple of them sense the captain's agitation and keep their attention focused. They break away from the group and walk towards the railing. When they get there, they look down at the hull of their ship where the captain has been pointing.

Their eyes widen in horror.

Like people waking up from a dream in a house that's on fire, they finally see the danger.

Their ship is sinking and if they do not do something right now, they are going to die.

They gasp for air.

They look at each other.

They fight the panic that threatens to overwhelm their reason.

They take a few deep breaths.

They assess the situation and they realize there is hope.

"There are lifeboats on this ship, and there's another ship close by," one says.

"Everything is going to be OK," says another.

"We just have to find the captain of our ship," they exclaim and as they realize this, they bolt towards the front of their sinking vessel. They run as fast as they can, climbing stairs, until finally they burst through the bridge doors where they find, to their utter horror and confusion, a totally empty bridge.

Their mouths drop to the floor.

"Where's the captain?" they gasp.

"Where's the crew?"

They pause for a few moments, turning in dazed circles, before they stop, look at each other, and bolt out of the room.

"We have to find the captain," they exclaim as they dash down towards the decks. Thankfully, it does not take them long. After only a few moments of searching, they find the captain surrounded by a big crowd of people, lounging around at the bow of the boat.

They run up and try to talk with him.

They notice he is drunk.

They begin shaking and slapping him.

He struggles under the blows for a moment and then abruptly finds his composure and brushes them away.

"What is the meaning of this," he bellows as he turns to look for security.

The two who were hitting him point to the railing. In disgust, the captain walks over to the railing, sees the new ship, looks at her captain, looks at his hull, and quietly turns pale as a ghost. He looks over at the captain of the new boat who, seeing that the other captain is finally aware of the danger, is already running back to his own bridge to stop his ship. The captain of the old ship understands immediately. He turns to the other two and says, "We can't use the lifeboats unless we stop the ship". You watch as the captain of the sinking ship bolts back to the bridge. He bursts into the room and gives the order. He stands there for a moment, waiting to be sure the ship is slowing and then, when he is satisfied, he runs back down to the deck. He finds the two who originally alerted him and together they find the nearest lifeboat and they begin shouting and trying to shake up the "sleeping" people.

"Wake up, wake up, wake up!" they say, "The ship we're on is sinking!" Shocked, they find their shouting and shaking has almost no effect. The people on the sinking ship simply are not listening. In fact, they do not seem to care at all. What is worse, they seem to be resisting. In fact, the more agitated the captain gets, and the louder the panicked calls to awaken become, the more resistant they become. But the captain and the others don't give up. They do not stop trying. How can they? The ship is sinking and besides, they can see that the captain of the new ship has already stopped his vessel and has lowered all his lifeboats. Everything is ready. If they can just get these people to wake up, everything will be OK.

Desperately they run from group to group trying to wake people up, trying to get them to notice. They grow weary of pushing through crowds and tired of all the resistance, but they stick at it and they do make progress. A few people here and there wake up and realize their ship is sinking; and of course, their reaction is predictable. When they finally see the state of their ship, when they finally realize that the ship is sinking and there is nothing they can do, they start to panic. Some scream, some grasp at their families, some begin weeping, and some snap under the fear and lose control; but in most cases the disorientation and panic does not last long. The captain and his crew are standing by reassuring everyone, pointing to the lifeboats, and repeating over and over, "There's enough time to save everyone". The message slowly gets through to them. They're scared and they know there's a danger; but, as they see the truth of the situation, as they see the lifeboats in the water and the captain of the new ship waiting to take them aboard, a calmness passes over them and a few begin orderly movement towards the lifeboats.

You breathe a sigh of relief because people are slowly waking up and it looks like everything might be OK after all. Still, and quite curiously, you can see that most of the people who wake up do not immediately begin moving to the lifeboats. In fact, even though they have the opportunity, most stay behind to help. It does not take you long to figure out why. They have family, friends, and children after all. They have a responsibility to others and they want to help; and that is great because even though the exodus has begun, the vast majority of the people on the old ship are still oblivious to the reality of their impending doom, and they are still locked in their delusional party mode. That is a problem because even with a growing army of determined workers it is slow going. People continue to ignore the warnings, resist, and lash out.

That is when you begin to worry again. People are waking up, but they are not waking up fast enough. With a worried look on your face, you scan the water line and that is when you notice that "it" has started to happen. Finally, the old ship has sunk so low in the water that its top deck is now at water level. Now, the bow of the boat dips gently below the waves and water comes splashing up onto the deck, soaking the feet of the revelers. When that happens, when their feet begin to get wet, they can no longer ignore the situation. Pausing, they look at the ship and they realize, finally, that something is terribly wrong. When that happens, when the collective realization of impending doom sweeps the ship, things change dramatically. Like a little emotional atom bomb pushed into a chain reaction, the sudden and ship-wide realization of imminent disaster sends energetic ripples cascading throughout the sinking ship and it literally explodes with fear. Standing back from the ship you can sense how momentous it is. The energy from the fear is raw and potent, like nothing you have ever experienced before, and you are certain that it will spell doom for those on the ship.

You know exactly what is coming!

Fear will ascend to panic will ascend to horror, there will be mass panic, and the people will go down with the ship. As these thoughts flow through your head, you look over at the ship expecting to see chaos, but are surprised to find none. Instead, you see orderly movement and controlled evacuation. You ask yourself, "How can this be?" And then you see the reason. Not only do lifeboats from the new ship surround the sinking old ship, but no sooner do people wake up and panic than there is somebody there to calm them and direct them to the nearest boat. You can still feel the energetic ripple of fear, but the energy never manifests into the descending spiral of panic and chaos that you expect. The ubiquitous lifeboats and the kindhearted individuals who stayed behind ensure that all the passengers from the old boat are safely transported to the new. Time passes and the rescue operations continue. Finally, just as the sun begins to set on the remains of the decrepit old ship, you see the last of the survivors lifted to the new ship. They stand on the deck watching the final moments of the derelict old ship as it sinks silently beneath the waves. Peace, serenity, and joy wash over the people on the ship. You smile. Their ordeal is over. A new journey, and a new world, lay spread out before them on the beautiful, still glass ocean.

Winnowing the Wheat

Discernment, discernment, discernment.

If you have been browsing the web or reading spiritual materials, chances are you have heard the phrase "use your discernment". It comes up quite a bit amongst spiritual types, often in the form of a disclaimer. You will be reading this channeled author or that spiritual website and at some point, you will come across some statement saying that whatever was said on the website, whatever was typed or YoutTubed, whatever opinions were expressed were just that, opinion. In the final analysis, you the reader should "use your discernment". This means you need to winnow the wheat from the chaff and decide for yourself whether the information is true or not, useful or not, liberating or not.

That is discernment!

It is a good sentiment, and good advice. You certainly do want to use your discernment, especially when you read spiritual information. If you want to wake up, if you want to make consistent and constant spiritual progress forward, if you do not want to experience setbacks, awakening failures, or even psychological pathologies, and if you want to *awaken, activate, and ascend* you, definitely want to be careful about what sorts of ideas, concepts, and archetypes you are putting into your head. You definitely want to discern, otherwise you could run into trouble. Let me be as clear and blunt as possible with you. If you put conceptual and ideological nonsense into your brain, you will do one or more of the following toxic things; you will:

- Create conditions for **Disjuncture**,[2] thus making it harder for Consciousness to enter into The Vessel.[3]

- Manifest conditions of hierarchy, dysfunction, and resistance to your own (and others) awakening and activation.

- Exacerbate underlying mental issues and pathology and, in the worst of cases, possibly

---

[2] **Disjuncture** is a key Lightning Path term. The term refers to the emotional and psychological stress that arises when the Physical Unit is "out of alignment" with its Resident Monadic Consciousness. Disjuncture arises when there is a disconnect between what Consciousness wants and what is actually happening in the material world around you. For more, see the SpiritWiki entry at http://www.thespiritwiki.com/Disjuncture. Also see Sharp, Lightning Path Workbook Three - Foundations.

For a definition of **Alignment** and **Resident Monadic Consciousness**, http://www.thespiritwiki.com/Alignment and http://www.thespiritwiki.com/Resident_Monadic_Consciousness.

[3] The vessel is another term for the physical body or the physical unit in LP nomenclature. It is a word selected when you wish to emphasize the physical body as a container (i.e. vessel) for higher Consciousness. For more, see http://www.thespiritwiki.com/The_Vessel/.

even get yourself medicated and committed.

And that is only an overview of what can go wrong. If you want to awaken, activate, and ascend, you really do have to be careful. If you want to move forward, you have to learn to discern!

Now, under healthy conditions discernment would not be a problem. Under healthy conditions our parents, teachers, media, and schools (i.e. our societies' **Agents of Consciousness**[4] and **Agents of Socialization**[5]) would teach us the truth about things and we would grow up knowing the difference between piles of disempowering, dogmatic BS and sparkles of empowering spiritual truths. As the result of a healthy socialization process, our physical vehicle would naturally become a vessel for higher Consciousness, we

---

[4] An Agent of Consciousness is an agent of socialization whose specific purpose is to insert ideas and Archetypes into the individual and Collective Consciousness of this planet. Writers, directors, advertising agents, school teachers, parents, news reporters, university professors, and any other individual involved in the transmission of archetypes through song, dance, news, education, etc., may be considered an Agent of Consciousness. For more on this important topic, see http://www.thespiritwiki.com/Agents_of_Consciousness/.

[5] An Agent of Socialization is an individual or institution tasked with the replication of the Social Order. An Agent of Socialization is responsible for transferring the rules, expectations, norms, values, and folkways of a given social order. http://www.thespiritwiki.com/Agents_of_Socialization/.

would naturally grow up accepting our divinity, we would smoothly connect with our own higher Consciousness, Consciousness would flow naturally into the body, and we would automatically be able to discern. Unfortunately, we do not live in such healthy conditions. The reality is, we are born and grow up in spiritually toxic conditions. These toxic conditions provide neither the framework for the full expression of our Consciousness nor the psychological, emotional, or intellectual foundations for stronger **Connection.**[6] The truth is, on this Earth we experience various levels of psychological, emotional, social, physical, political, and economic toxicity, and various depths of untruth and lie. As a result, our **Physical Unit**[7] (i.e. our body and mind) fails to mature properly and subsequently fails to express the conscious, compassionate, and discerning light beings that we really are. This failure to mature is a problem not only because an improperly nurtured and matured physical unit cannot properly connect with and express the full

---

[6] Connection is the Lightning Path term for what occurs when the bodily ego unites with higher Consciousness. When the bodily ego unites with higher consciousness we may say the body has made a connection to Consciousness. Connection is the holy grail of spiritual practice and the point and purpose of Lightning Path spirituality. See http://www.thespiritwiki.com/Connection.

[7] The term Physical Unit is the Lightning Path term for your physical body. The physical unit includes both your physical body (arms, legs, muscles, organs) and your body's central nervous systems functions, for example your body's sense of ego, and your body's autonomic physiological responses. For more see http://www.thespiritwiki.com/Physical_Unit.

power and divine light of its own higher Consciousness, but also because *an improperly matured physical unit cannot be relied upon to tell the truth about anything broaching God, Consciousness, and Creation.* Improperly matured physical units cannot connect with Consciousness and cannot realize nor tell the truth, and this is for three basic reasons.

First, you cannot rely on truths uttered by spiritually immature physical units because the individual may simply not understand. When operating with limited Consciousness it is very difficult to understand even the most basic spiritual truths. Even people with clear connections often express difficulty.[8] I have to say, limited Consciousness means limited understanding. Couple limited understanding with a developmentally damaged ego and you make realization and expression of high spiritual truths well-nigh impossible. Getting lucid, meaningful, accurate, and pure statements about spiritual truths from somebody who has experienced **Toxic Socialization**[9] and never healed from it is like

---

[8] Mystics the world over often express difficulty and frustration when trying to understand and express high spiritual truths. In fact it is so common that scientists who study the process put down "ineffability" as a standard feature of the mystical experience. When a mystic says their experience is ineffable, they mean they can't describe it in words.

[9] Toxic Socialization is a socialization process specifically designed to fracture attachments, undermine Self Esteem, destroy ego boundaries, and disable the body's ability to contain higher levels of Consciousness. For more, see the SpiritWiki entry http://www.thespiritwiki.com/Toxic_Socialization.

trying to get a statement of reality from somebody babbling in their sleep. Not only are they obviously not paying attention to anything you might be thinking, but they are babbling randomly about disjointed ideas occurring in the dream space of their minds. That might be interesting to a psychologist, but only a fool would go to a drooling sleeper asking for spiritual advice and truth. If you do that, if you pay attention to half-cocked babblings of the disconnected spiritual sleeper, the only thing you are going to get is confused. Therefore, if you want to make forward progress you need to learn to recognize when a sleeper is babbling spiritual nonsense. In other words, learn to discern spiritually mature teachers from immature, half-cocked, sleepers.

Second, there is the issue of indoctrination. If you have been following along any type of **Authentic Spiritual Pathway,**[10] and especially if you have been following along with Lightning Path spirituality, then by now you will fully realize we are all victims of deep indoctrination. As explained in some detail in my *Book of the Triumph of Spirit* series, **Archetypes**[11] are ideas

---

[10] Authentic Spirituality is spirituality that leads to connection with Consciousness. For more, see http://www.thespiritwiki.com/Authentic_Spirituality. Also Michael Sharp, The Rocket Scientists' Guide to Authentic Spirituality (St. Albert, Alberta: Lightning Path Press, 2010). Also see Sharp, Lightning Path Workbook Two - Introduction to the Lightning Path.

[11] An archetype is any conscious or unconscious idea that

designed to make us docile and compliant, impotent and confused, archetypes which I call **Old Energy Archetypes**[12], are inserted into **Bodily Consciousness**[13] starting at birth. These archetypes come to corrupt our awareness and understanding at profound levels. The corruption is so bad that the people of this Earth, people who are in essence compassionate and loving "star" beings, have no difficulty justifying, ignoring, and even contributing to hate, war, poverty, greed, starvation, and so on. Remarkably, *our thinking is so corrupted that some people even think that we deserve all the suffering and violence on this Earth,* that it is necessary, that it is "good for us", or that all the suffering and violence we experience is part of some divine cosmic "lesson plan". To these people this planet is a kind of spiritual schoolhouse where God/Gaia punishes us for our (karmic) sins, teaches us

---

provides an individual or collective answer to a big question, like "Who am I?" or "Why am I here?" Archetypes can be visual, linguistic, and even musical.

For more see http://www.thespiritwiki.com/Archetypes. Also check out my *Book of the Triumph of Spirit* series. For details, visit http://press.thelightningpath.com/.

[12] Old Energy Archetypes are archetypes designed to disconnect the bodily ego from Consciousness and deactivate/damage the physical unit. Old energy archetypes suppress Consciousness in various ways and prevent it from descending into the physical unit. For more, see http://www.thespiritwiki.com/Old_Energy_Archetypes.

[13] Bodily Consciousness, which can be distinguished from Spiritual consciousness, is the un-insightful, autonomic, physiologically rooted "consciousness" of your physical body. http://www.thespiritwiki.com/Bodily_Consciousness/.

our (karmic) lessons, and then promotes and rewards the "chosen" ones who "deserve" it. Of course, it is ridiculous to think that we need or deserve pain, suffering, poverty, hunger, violence and war, or that these experiences are part of some divine lesson plan, or that Consciousness "promotes" some and discards (or burns) others, but people believe it anyway. These beliefs permeate the conceptual space of this planet and corrupt the spiritual truths we are exposed to. That is a problem. If you put the half-truths, partial deceptions, and outright lies wittingly or unwittingly propagated by individuals soaked in the toxic ideological gunk of this planet into your brain, you will never make progress forward on The Path. Therefore, you have to learn to discern truth from indoctrination.

Failure to understand caused by limited Consciousness in body and failure to understand caused by indoctrination at the hands of **System Agents**[14] makes it difficult to sort the wheat from the chaff. There is a **third** reason that makes discernment practice even more challenging and more important and this is the fact that many people actively work at deception. The truth is there are many people out there who are paid, and very well I might add, to mislead you. How many is impossible to tell, but if you have spent any time

---

[14] A System Agent is an individual who works, with more or less clarity, to maintain and reproduce The System. See http://www.thespiritwiki.com/System_Agents/.

listening to teachers, preachers on television or the Internet, you will have come across somebody trying to teach you ideas with the specific intent of sowing confusion, encouraging **Disjuncture**,[15] and lowering Consciousness in the body. And just in case you are not paying attention, let me say it again. Many people out there deliberately lie in order to ensure you remain asleep and impotent. These people know what **The System**[16] is about (i.e. it is about control), they know (or vaguely suspect) the interests they work for, and they deliberately try to deceive and mislead, and not always for nefarious reasons. Although it is true that some people are fully aware that the lies they teach disconnect, confuse, and thereby prop up and support the status quo and the System, not everybody is so aware of whom they really serve. In fact, most people are not. *Many people deliberately lie not because they are self-consciously greedy or "evil", but because they think it is the right thing to do.* They did not use

---

[15] Disjuncture is the emotional and psychological stress that arises when the physical unit is out of alignment with its Resident Monadic Consciousness. Disjuncture arises when there is a disconnect between what Consciousness wants its body to do, and what the body is actually doing. The ideas in your head can encourage disjuncture. For example, if you think it is OK to yell at your children, you will be much more likely engage in this profoundly abusive, and deeply damaging, emotional torture. http://www.thespiritwiki.com/Disjuncture.

[16] For more on The System, what it is, and what it is all about, see Michael Sharp, The Rocket Scientists' Guide to Money and the Economy: Accumulation and Debt. (St Albert, Alberta: Lightning Path Press., 2016).

discernment, they just blindly follow. They believe it is the right thing to do because their masters and handlers have told them it is so by seeding one or more of the following lies:

- That the "sheep" need to be tended.

- That they are doing "God's" evolutionary and/or moral work.

- That it is part of the cosmic plan.

- That it is the "natural" order of things.

- That the masses must be controlled otherwise disaster would result.

- That they are the ones "chosen" to lead.

They do it, in essence, because they have been told, and they eventually tell themselves, it is the right thing to do. *They believe and so they deceive.* But, whatever; it doesn't matter why people work for "the man" or why they choose to support the System; what is important is that rich or poor, black or white, high or low, male or female you realize that because of all the blindfolded,[17] confused, indoctrinated, and deceptive

---

[17] To say that people are blindfolded is to say they have a veil over their consciousness, or that they are sleeping in a spiritual coma, or that they have a low CQ. The term The Blindfold is a metaphoric term used by Michael Sharp to refer to the limitations of Consciousness that occur as a result of the Toxic

people out there, you have to discern. It is like being lost in the woods and taking direction from somebody else who is also lost in the woods, but does not realize they are lost. If you do that, you are going nowhere, fast. If you do that, you will eventually die in the woods.

Just to recap, if spiritual awakening is your goal then you have to learn how to discern. You have to learn to winnow the wheat (i.e. information that will keep you moving forward) from the chaff (i.e. information that will halt your forward progress). What is more, you have to do it now because, as anybody with eyes can see, the old world, your old world, is falling apart and there is no more time to waste.

Unfortunately, while learning to discern is a critical thing for anybody who is serious about making stronger connections with Consciousness, learning to discern is not as simple as saying to yourself "I am not going to be fooled again". Confusion, indoctrination, and intentional deception make winnowing the wheat, as Christ said, or distinguishing the "Real from the unreal" as Adi Shankara said in the Vivekachudamani, difficult. Still, if you are sinking in a sea of spiritual disinformation and you want to find your way to shore

---

Socialization endured by humans living under the emotional, psychological, spiritual, and economic yoke of The System. For more details see www.thespiritwiki.com/The_Blindfold. To get a better idea of the implications, read my *Parable of the Blindfold.* http://www.michaelsharp.org/parable-of-the-blindfold/.

then, bottom line, you are going to have to learn to discern. The question at this point is, what do you do and how do you get started?

INTENT AND EXPECTATION

Well, there are a few things you can do, and a few things you can look for, that will help you get started. **The first thing** you have to do is quit settling for half-truth and lies. Do not listen to Disney on this one. Do not "let it go". Instead of "letting it go", learn to expect, nay demand, the truth and nothing but the truth no compromise and no strings attached.[18]

Expect it. Expect it! Expect it!

Why? Simply because expectation is a very important part of what I am going to call **Creation's Equation**.[19] In

---

[18] The meaning of no compromise should be obvious, the meaning of "no strings attached" a little more obtuse. The sub phrase "no strings attached" means you should get the truth without also being subject to manipulation and control. Lots of people offer the truth these days, but often it comes with puppet strings (e.g. advertising, social and emotional control, intellectual manipulations, etc.). Fair exchange is one thing, sacrificing yourself and your soul just to get a little truth is another thing altogether. My advice to you is, don't do it. You have a right to the truth and nothing but, no compromise and no strings attached.

[19] Creation's Equation is a mnemonic that abstractly describes the deep process of creation. Creation's equation is a statement of the fundamental mechanic of creation. Creation's equation may be stated simply as *force + formation = creation*. For more,

order to understand why expectation is important, how it fits into Creation's Equation, and how it all works, you have to recall the basic *Lightning Path* principle *as above in consciousness, so below in matter.*[20] This principle states that what is in consciousness eventually gets manifested in the world around you. The question is, how is consciousness manifested in creation? I talk about the basics of this in my book *The Great Awakening: Concepts and Techniques for Successful Spiritual Practice.*[21] There I say that consciousness is manifested in reality through a process of *intent and visualization.* In that book I say that if you want things to happen you have to intend and visualize, and that is certainly true. Put more formally we could say that if you want things to happen, you have to manifest using Creation's Equation. Creation's equation is

Force + Formation = Creation

In the above equation, Force (a.k.a. intent) is coupled with Formation (a.k.a. expectation) to give you Creation. In other words, if you want to create something you apply force, give that force a form, and *voila,* you have creation. Of course, you probably

---

see http://www.thespiritwiki.com/Creations_Equation/.

[20] You could also say *energy goes where consciousness flows,* reality follows vision, energy follows intent, and/or matter mirrors expectation

[21] I go deeper in Michael Sharp, <u>The Book of Life: Ascension and the Divine World Order</u> (St. Albert, AB: Lightning Path Press/Avatar Publications, 2003).

already know about the importance of intent in regards to creation and manifestation. These days, and thanks to the ideologues behind the *Law of Attraction,* everybody and their dog know about intent. However, though you may be aware of the importance of intent (which is force), you may not have considered the importance of expectation (which is formation). Intent is certainly important, but expectation is critical. Indeed, expectation is more important than intent! This is not because expectation is privileged over intent; they both represent key aspects of the flow of consciousness. The difference that makes expectation more important (and stronger, it should be noted) than intent is that expectation operates 100 percent of the time. Unlike intent that operates and exerts pressure only when you are paying attention, expectations operate consciously when you are thinking about your expectations, and unconsciously even when your attention and will are elsewhere. Expectations exert creative pressure on the *energies* of reality full time. You can be sleeping and expectation continues to bear force. It is this "constant on" feature of formation/expectation that makes expectation much more potent than intent!

It is true.

Formative expectation diffused throughout **The Fabric**

of Consciousness[22] *at all levels is a critical component of manifestation and creation.*

This is why so much effort goes into degrading and controlling the expectations of the masses.[23] It is also why archetypes and ideas are so important.[24] Expectation is manipulated and controlled via the implantation of archetypes! If you want to create a world of duality and violence where the strong (who are "good") bash on the weak (who are "evil") implant and then reinforce (like Marvel Studios and much of Hollywood) archetypes of good fighting evil.

Simple!

If you teach people to expect a world of good fighting evil, this is what they will accept as valid reality, and this

---

[22] The term Fabric of Consciousness is a term I coined in 2003 while writing *The Book of Light*. The term is a non-denominational and syncretic representation of the sum total of Consciousness as it exists. For more, see Sharp, The Book of Life: Ascension and the Divine World Order.

[23] Indeed, mass expectation is carefully controlled on this planet. The masses are taught to expect products, services, new fads, and a constantly churning supply of Hollywood pretty people designed to divert and distract. Compare these degraded expectations with higher alternatives like the expectation of peace, prosperity, love, support, nurturing, and even healing, all of which we are taught not to expect! I have to say, this world would be a much different place if our expectations were not debased to serve the economic and political goals of the elites.

[24] And it's why I spend so much time unpacking "old energy" archetypes and elaborating "new energy" archetypes in *The Book of the Triumph of Spirit* series.

is what they will create via the force of their magical intent, and the formation of their daily actions (or inactions, as the case may be). Likewise, if you want to create a world of privilege and power where the "beautiful people" who are worthy of reward lord it over, laugh, and control the unworthy (or those deserving of judgment and punishment), simply implant and reinforce archetypes of judgment, reward, punishment, and control. If you expect life is a war between good and evil, if you think life is an unending evolutionary struggle played out on a checkerboard of black and white, if you think some people deserve to have billions of dollars while millions of children deserve to starve and die, then you will contribute to the *formation* of a world in line with your expectations. You get/create what you expect. Most importantly, what you expect is determined by the ideas and archetypes in your brain!

It is very important you understand this, because not only is expectation important in all areas of your life, expectation is particularly important when it comes to discernment. This is because, just like intent and expectation help determine the types of things we manifest in creation, *intent and expectation also influence and determine the types of truths we receive, accept, and generate as well.* If you expect that humans are incapable of understanding the deep mysteries of creation, that is what you will get—humans who cannot understand. If you expect confusion and disorientation, do not be surprised when you find and accept prophets who speak only in riddles, and who sow (wittingly or unwittingly) confusion in your day.

The key is EXPECTATION.

You get, and create, what you expect.

Do you want to change this reality? Do you want to triumph over confusion? Do you want to alter your life? Do you want to end suffering (yours and others)? Then, quit compromising your expectations. Set your standards as high as you can imagine (I like to say, "Expect the truth and nothing but, no compromise and no strings attached") and then expect only the best, brightest, highest, and most lucid truths there can be.

Expect nothing less than the highest good for all.

Expect nothing less than the expansion of full Consciousness into the vehicle.

Expect nothing less than the full and empowered connection with God.

This is very important! Until we change our expectations, stop compromising our goals, stop accepting the world "as it is," and start demanding a world "as it should be", until we all work together to create the expectation of truth and utopia, the old world and everything in it, including the spiritual confusion of this planet, will continue to exist. You get what you expect. If you want to change the world, change your expectations immediately.

ISSUES AND CHALLENGES

Perhaps this all makes a certain degree of intuitive sense, but setting high expectations can be a bit harder than you might at first think, and this is for several reasons. **First of all**, and as perverse as it might sound, *when it comes to spirituality and religion we are all trained to accept half-truths.* As you read this, you may be thinking this is just jest. Who but a fool willingly accepts half-truths and lies? Unfortunately, it is the case, at least when it comes to religion and spirituality, that many people do indeed accept half-truths and lies. I know I did. For the longest time I believed that it would not be possible to ever know with any degree of certainty the spiritual or cosmological truths of creation. Over the years, I have heard many people say the same thing. I believed at one time, as so many others still do, that humans are just too limited, and Consciousness just too grand to think we would ever be able to sort it all out. I was speaking to a woman the other day who said, in defense of her own flawed spirituality, that all belief systems are flawed and that there was no way we could ever know the whole truth. She truly believed that all spiritual systems were incomplete and had error in them and therefore no belief system had any sort of monopoly or claim to truth. Put another way, she felt it did not matter who you talked to or what you did, you would always have to accept some limited version of truth. According to her, it would only be by some divine act of grace that we would ever escape the dark.

She had, as you can see, very low expectations; and, is not that the way a lot of us think, at least when it comes to spiritual truths? Do we not believe that no individual and/or no spiritual system will ever be able tell us the truth, the whole truth, and nothing but the truth? Do we not believe that all systems are flawed, all truths are partial, and all spiritualities are limited? Do we not accept, on principle, the limited, confusing, and spiritually "dark" nature of Earthly existence? It is true, we do,[25] and when we do, we naturally lower our expectations. Obviously, that has to stop. Instead of assuming that lowly humans cannot know the ineffable truths of creation, we must accept it is possible and expect that we can achieve it. As long as we think we cannot, we cannot. If we believe we cannot accomplish it, we will never even try.

Of course, believing that humans are weak, pathetic, and incapable of knowing the truth is not the only reason we lower our expectations *vis à vis* the truth. In addition to being trained to lower our expectations, **the second reason** we lower expectations is for political reasons. Many people have been burned by spiritualities that claim a monopoly on salvation and truth, yet proffer nothing but oppression, suppression,

---

[25] And note, it is not just the "common folk" who think this way either. I know scientists, philosophers, psychologists, sociologists, and others members of the academy who take on principle the complex, confusing, and "ineffable" nature of creation.

and violence. As a result, many people are rightly gun shy when it comes to the strong epistemological claims of some religions. Take the Catholic religion for example. It claims to provide ultimate truth, yet it represents one of the most violent and oppressive[26] institutions on the planet, burning women, raping children,[27] and serving up darkness and confusion for centuries. On the other hand, consider Islam. The Prophet, peace be unto him, professes to speak *"In the name of Allah, the Beneficent, the Merciful",*[28] yet his words (if they are his words) come tinged with encouragements toward copious shame and punishment.[29] Alternatively, consider the Vedic

---

[26] For a rundown of some of the oppressive and violent acts, as they are relevant in an LP context, see Sharp, The Book of Life: Ascension and the Divine World Order.

[27] By now we all know the Catholic Church's record and reaction to the revelation that their priests rape children.

[28] This phrase opens all one hundred and fourteen chapters of the Koran! I don't think it is unreasonable to suggest that the primary characteristics of Allah are beneficence and mercy and not bitter shame and anger.

[29] It is not worth denying this. The appeal to shame and punish others rings throughout the Koran. "Allah has set a seal upon their hearts and upon their hearing and there is a covering over their eyes, and there is a great punishment for them…. and they shall have a painful chastisement because they lied". Koran: 2.7-10. Also "Surely we have warned you of a chastisement near at hand: the day when man shall see what his two hands have sent before, and the unbeliever shall say: O! Would that I were dust!' Koran: 78.40. Does this mean we should reject the Koran as an expression of the Word, or Muhammad as an authentic prophet of God? Absolutely not. I just think we have to be aware that Muhammad did not write the words down himself, somebody

spiritualities of India. Vedic spiritualities are arguably the most sophisticated attempts to understand Consciousness on the planet, yet some if it (how much I do not know) comes wrapped in a blatant and remarkably oppressive social-class tinged patriarchy.[30] The list of religion's sins would fill volumes, and indeed it has.[31] It is hard for anybody with even nascent awareness to ignore these obvious failures! In an environment where so many big religious traditions offer half-baked lies and rotten untruths, people find it hard to expect much.[32]

Who can blame them? After being disappointed so many times, they just give up in frustration and say, "we'll never know the whole spiritual truth, so why even

---

else did. It is very possible that the words were interfered with in the process of transcription, duplication, and transmission.

[30] For example, it is written in the Vivekachudamani that a "male body" is rare and precious and it is implied that it is the most highly sought after vehicle.

[31] And indeed has. See the four volumes by Ellens as an example J. Harold Ellens, The Destructive Power of Religion: Violence in Judaism, Christianity, and Islam

ed. J. Harold Ellens, vol. 1, 4 vols. (Westport, CT: Praegar, 2001).

[32] Don't get me wrong here. There is much beauty and truth to be found in the words of all the authentic prophets of this planet, but the texts are old and they are typically written by somebody other than the prophet themselves, and they have passed through many dirty, greedy, hands and minds along their way to you. The words of the prophets have been scathed by their journey through darkness. If you want my opinion, no traditional religious text is above reproach.

bother to try". There is not much I can say to that. If you want to give up, feel free. However, if you are interested in a loftier goal, do not give up. If you (if we) want the truth, the whole truth, and nothing but the truth we have to find it for ourselves. We can do that, but the only way we can do that is to put aside our disillusion and disappointment with the big traditions, wade in, and find the truth for ourselves. The first step in that direction is to raise our expectations and believe it is possible. If we do not believe it is possible to find the truth, we will not even bother to try.

Believing that it is not possible to know the truth, and giving up for political reasons (i.e. with the big traditions), are two reasons people lower their expectation when it comes to truth. **A third reason** people lower their expectations is because *lowered expectations give you an easy way out* if, for some reason, you don't want to try too hard. Perhaps you are beaten and weak. Perhaps you are tired or alone. Perhaps you are frustrated and scared. Perhaps you have no time or energy. Perhaps you cannot "handle" the truth. Perhaps there is a bit of a struggle here. Perhaps it will take some work. Perhaps it is a challenge for you and perhaps you feel like you are not up to the challenge. If this is so, that is OK! No worries! It is hard, so go ahead and settle for half-truths and lies. After all, nobody speaks the whole truth, nobody can ever understand it all, and it is all relative anyway, so why try too hard? Just cherry pick what does not challenge too much and be happy with that in the end.

Sit back and relax!

Don't worry, be happy.

Questions, concerns, doubts, fears, challenges, and the sometimes hard work of moving forward can be easily swept aside with a simple "well, it is all flawed anyway so I'll just stick with what I got" shtick. It comes down to this; *if you do not expect so much when it comes to spiritual truth, you do not have to try so hard to find it.*

Of course, if that is your choice what can I say? If you want to give up in frustration or take the easy way out, feel free. There is nothing particularly wrong with that, and certainly nobody is going to judge you in the end. All I will say here is, it gets easier. It can seem hard at the beginning, but if you stick with it, and if pride does not prevent you from admitting you are wrong or finding help when you need it, it gets easier pretty quickly. If you want my advice, do not give up and do not take the easy way out. Demand the truth and nothing but. Demand the truth with a capital "T". It is the only way forward.

Believing humans are too limited to understand, political frustration, and taking an easy way out are three reasons you might settle for less than perfect truth. **A fourth reason** you might feel it is OK to lower expectations is that low expectations allow you to avoid your responsibility to others, including your children. Saying that "truth is relative", that "all paths lead home", or "they'll find their own way" allows you to wash your hands of responsibility. Lowering expectations makes it easy to say, "it is not my responsibility", "I don't know what's going on", or "you have to figure it out for yourself". You may find it hard to believe anybody would want to do that, but consider that finding the truth, applying the truth, being the truth, and finally fighting for the truth can be a lot of hard work. You can avoid all the struggle, conflict, work, and responsibility that comes when you align yourself with truth and consciousness by simply lowering your standards and expectations and settling for less than you are capable. It seems horrible, especially when you realize the real sacrifice,[33] but it is done all the time. People, even parents, often would rather selfishly immerse themselves in their own self-absorbed pursuits and addictions than assume responsibility for others. Taking the selfish way out they then justify it to themselves (and others) by having low expectations and low standards. Moving forward, aligning yourself with Consciousness, and taking responsibility can require much work, and it can take deep commitment, but lowering expectations and standards means you don't have to do the work after all.

Consider a family we knew. Consider a mother and a father, toxic beyond all belief. Consider a child

---

[33] The real sacrifice is the sacrifice of Self, with a capital "S". Self with a capital "S" refers to your higher self, or spiritual ego. See http://www.thespiritwiki.com/Self/.

swimming in the toxicity of the family and struggling with decades of abuse. Consider that the child breaks down in his early twenties, becomes unstable, and enters psychosis. Consider his parents reaction. Rather than do the hard work of taking ownership, changing their expectations, and repairing their damaged family, they find distraction, make excuses, and wash their hands. Of course, they make it look like they are doing something. The dad works harder at work and the mom, on her way to a self-care appointment, hands her child some new age book she has not even read. It does not matter that the poor boy is struggling with psychosis; she just does not have the time for him. She tells herself he will figure it out on his own. Problem solved! Now she can enjoy her life with the peace of mind that comes from knowing she did everything she possibly could.

And isn't it easier this way! Handing him the book and letting him "figure it out" allows her to focus on herself. By lowering her expectations, she can wash her hands and absolve herself of responsibility. Obviously, this isn't the best way to do things. By busying themselves with other things, the parents fail to address the root causes of the psychosis (their own selfish toxicity) and fail to properly vet and support their son's struggle to regain sanity. The consequences of their failure were dire. As the young man explored the book that his undiscerning mother had given him, his instability increased. He lit their house on fire and was arrested and thrown into a psych ward where he was diagnosed and chemically straightjacketed. To be fair, the horrible materials she handed to him were not the only cause of his breakdown. It was ultimately the abuse in his family that damaged his mental structures and made him susceptible to psychosis, but damage can be repaired if properly treated. Repairing damage requires that individuals and families take ownership, assume responsibility, and work! Sadly, it is much easier to lower expectations and settle for the emotional and psychological status quo. When we do, the negative consequences can be profound, but as is the case with this family, you can always delude yourself that there is no better way, there is nothing you can do, and that everybody got what they deserved. The reality is that this young man's mom and dad abused and neglected him for decades and then, when he needed them most, they absolved themselves of responsibility and, through their undiscerning actions, led him into the wilderness where he stumbled and fell. By the end of it all, his family had completely avoided ownership and was embracing his illness as divine providence. Now they do not call him the mentally ill son, they call him the "family muse".

And the moral of the story is? We lower our expectations to absolve ourselves of our responsibility to others. If "anything goes", if "we all find our own path", and "if it's up to you to discern for yourself", then we have no problem just standing around and being stupid while the people around us drown. It is horrible to think, but it happens all the time. Once again, there is not much I can say to that. If you want to give up in frustration, take the easy way out, or accept the status quo so that you can absolve yourself of responsibility, feel free. All I will say is *Consciousness is responsible for everything.* If you are not responsible, you are simply not conscious. If Consciousness is your goal, find the highest Light, seek the highest truth, and take responsibility for Creation.

A fifth reason that we lower expectation is because of the oppressive impact of victimization. The truth of our reality on this Earth is that those who are stronger, more powerful, and more violent victimize many people. Parents and teachers victimize children; intimate partners and coworkers victimize parents; corporations, armies, and police victimize people. This victimization, whatever it is, causes people to lower their expectations. The problem is that *victimization teaches people that they have no power.* When an adult hurts, hits, or even rapes a child, the child learns that they have no power to stop things. When a worker is exploited, harassed, or otherwise assaulted by a boss (or another employee), the worker learns they have no power to control their life. Individuals who experience constant victimization often simply give up trying to exert their will because they learn nothing they do makes any difference. As a result, they lower their expectations. If nothing they can say or do can make a difference, they learn powerlessness/helplessness.[34] It is a major problem for many people on this planet, and because of the psychological, emotional, and spiritual corruption/damage that it causes, it is not so easy to overcome (i.e. "attraction" just does not cut it). Space limitations prevent us from dealing with the negative outcomes or the potential solutions here, so it will have to suffice to note that lowered expectations because of chronic victimization is an important issue.

Now, believing humans are limited, finding an easy way out, giving up, absolving ourselves of responsibility, and victimization are five reasons we settle for half-baked, half-cocked spiritual truths. **A sixth and final reason** we lower our expectations is because a lackadaisical attitude towards truth allows us to avoid necessary confrontation and challenge. This is an issue because confrontation and challenge is an aspect of the process of awakening and activation. *Confrontation and challenge is an inevitable outcome of authentic spirituality.* It comes in the form of challenges to yourself, your thinking, and your behavior for sure, but it also comes in the form of challenge and confrontation with others.

---

[34] In psychology the negative impact of chronic victimization was amply demonstrated by American psychologist Martin Seligman's *Learned Helplessness* experiments. An internet search will turn up a wealth of descriptive material on this important psychological/spiritual phenomenon.

It works like this.

As you awaken and activate you will inevitably bump up against the blindfolded ignorance and close-minded stupidity of those still wearing a blindfold. As you do you will find yourself driven to say something to them, to help enlighten their minds a bit, or move them forward a step or two. You will do this for several different reasons. You will do this for yourself because you may need them to change in order to support your own spiritual process (maybe they belittle you and you need them to stop). You will do this for them, hoping to help them move out and away from their own toxic darkness. You will also do this for the world, and in particular the children, so that all can benefit from the increasing expansion of light. You will be driven to do this because it is in the nature of who you are as an incarnated spark of divinity. You are Consciousness, Consciousness is Light[35], and Light dispels the darkness by simply being present. The truth is, if Consciousness is present, darkness cannot exist. Therefore, as Consciousness descends into your body you will feel increasingly compelled to shine a light and dispel the dark. As a result, you will necessarily be drawn into challenge and possibly conflict.

There is no other way!

Consciousness/God does not accept deception,

---

[35] Consciousness is Light, and Light is God.

disease, destruction, violence, and woe. Consciousness does not aid and abet. Consciousness shines a light. Consciousness dispels the dark, which is not a bad thing after all; however, because blindfolded people are, as a rule, defensive people, and because our approach to truth can be clumsy in the beginning, our challenge often triggers their defenses (or their guilt and shame), and they often react with aggression, even violence. *Despite our best, most gentle, and most loving intentions, shining a light on the world often invokes reaction, defensiveness, and conflict.* Of course, it does not have to be that way. Shining a light on the darkness, i.e. confronting somebody's delusions and illusions can be simple, non-combative, and even gentle. Indeed, shining the light and speaking the truth can be as simple as saying "I don't believe that, I believe this". Indeed these days speaking the truth can be as simple as tweeting ten words. Unfortunately, as easy as it can be, often it is not. As noted above, when you bring people to the truth, people are triggered and conflict often ensues. This is a big problem because most people do not like conflict, especially the emotionally, psychologically, and even physically violent way it is often played out on this world. Since shining a light leads to confrontation, since confrontation leads to conflict, and since most people don't like conflict, most people learn to avoid conflict by dimming their light, lowering their standards, and settling for the world "as it is".

We have all done it at one time or another. We have

all heard priests utter words designed to traumatize and scare children, yet we stand by and say nothing. We have all heard parents indoctrinating their child into the violent fundamentalisms of west and east, yet we stand by and say nothing. We have heard politicians issue lies as they support violence and greed, yet we stand by and say nothing. We have seen our loved ones follow paths of self-destruction, yet we stand by until it is far too late. It is easy to understand why we do this. We do this to avoid confrontation and conflict. Still, Consciousness is light and as Consciousness descends, Consciousness will shine a light, so you are going to have to get used to it. In an ideal world, it would not be an issue. In an ideal world, people would see the truth, and they would not be so defensive when challenged. Unfortunately, this is not an ideal world. Many are afraid to stand up, many are (legitimately) afraid of consequences and retaliation, and so in order to avoid conflict and soothe the painful feelings caused by their failure to shine a light, many lower their expectations and excuse themselves of the responsibility because it is a much easier way out of the situation.

Unfortunately, if you want to make spiritual progress, if you want to learn to discern, that is a problem. Sitting back and allowing toxicity and darkness to exist just because you are afraid of a little conflict is the same as enabling and abetting toxicity and darkness, and that will not fly with your higher Light. In an ideal and connected world, people stand up for the truth. In an ideal world, people challenge and uplift. I have to say this. *If you do not stand up for the Light then by default you work for the Dark.*

Now, I know this is a provocative statement, but it is true. People who stand in the Light stand up for the Truth, and not just on principle. There are important practical reasons why people do this. Consider a problem many of us are familiar with—addiction. If you have ever dealt with addictions you know one of the biggest obstacles to treating the addiction is getting rid of the enabling behavior in oneself and the ones that surround you. The hardest thing for families to realize is that if they want to help people with addiction, they have to stop enabling those addictions. When you have somebody addicted to gambling you cannot support that gambling in any way and you must challenge it at every turn, even if it causes conflict and family disconnection. When you do not do this, when you turn a blind eye to the fact that the behavior is obviously wrong, when you find excuses to justify its recurrence (perhaps by saying, "it is only his thing" or "he's just having a hard time at home" or "he's on vacation", etc.) you are enabling. If you fail to challenge because you are afraid of conflict you are allowing the destructive behavior to continue. If you are connected to an individual in some way and you fail to challenge, then their continued addiction is partly your fault.

Of course, you can tell yourself that is not true. You can pretend not to see the addiction (i.e. turn your light away), pretend it is not a problem even though it is, or tell yourself that it is not your responsibility. In other words, you can lower your expectations, and if you do that, fine. Just be honest with yourself. Do not tell yourself that it is OK, or that it is right, or that it is his choice, or that you have no right to expect. Tell yourself the truth. Be aware of your fears and anxieties; be aware of your limitations and failures; be aware of your excuses and justifications. Tell yourself the Truth! Say, "I know it is wrong, but I just haven't the strength", and be good with that. Sometimes you just have to leave it up to the professionals, and there is no shame in that. It is OK to bow out sometimes, just do not lower your standards or expectations if you do.

And that's all I have to say about intent, expectation, and the low standards of our modern world. Understand here that I am not saying these things to make you feel bad. The point is to highlight lowered expectations, show you why we accept them,[36] and encourage you to raise them. However, for reasons that should become clearer to you every day, we need to

---

[36] Remember, we are trained to accept lower standards, we avoid them for political reasons, we don't want to take responsibility, we think we are victims and therefore helpless, we prefer an easy way out, or we have fear of struggle and retaliation.

stop that. For the sake of God/Consciousness/Light, this planet, and the people who live on it, compromise has to stop and it has to stop now. The only way that is going to happen is if we raise expectations. The ship of the old world is sinking. If you do not want to go down with that ship then raise your expectations. *Demand the truth and nothing but, no compromise, and no strings attached.*

ACTIVATING YOUR INTERNAL BS DETECTOR

I hope that at this point you have been inspired to raise your expectations not only about finding and understanding the truth, but about other people's behavior as well. So what is next? Well, once you have raised your expectations, the next step is to use your brain and start finding the truth. The next step is to learn to discern. Unfortunately, this can be a bit of a problem not because discerning is inherently difficult (it is not) but because it is likely that nobody has ever taught you how to discern. The truth is, the System does not need fully awakened and activated spiritual beings; it needs slaves, peons, and people who are easy to control. For this reason and this reason only, they, and by "they" I mean agents of consciousness who work (advertently or inadvertently) for the System, do not teach discernment as part of a child's home or school curriculum.

Of course, it does not have to be this way. There is no spiritual reason for it and anybody who has ever observed children will know children are incredibly open, aware, intelligent, and inquiring. Because of the natural intelligence of the child, it is very easy to teach children to think critically, discern, create boundaries, and have high expectations. The problem is, "they" do not do it because "they" (and by "they" I mean the people in power) need us to be comatose, compliant, docile, and easy to manipulate. If "they" taught "us" (and by "us" I mean the children of this Earth) to see through all the BS, then as adults we would be a lot harder to manipulate and control.[37] While that might be good for me, my health, my family, and everybody else, it would be bad for the health and longevity of the System. *If everybody learned to discern right now, the System* (which, as should be increasingly obvious, is a dangerous hodgepodge of ideas and practices, for the planet), *would crumble overnight.* This is why critical thinking and discernment (especially spiritual discernment)[38] is not part of the K through 12

---

[37] For example, I taught my children about gender roles as soon as they could talk. I taught them about the mass media and its propagation of gender roles, I talked about consumerism and how corporations exploit gender to sell products. I talked about how boys and girls are treated differently just because they have different genitals. At the age of eleven and thirteen these two children are more sophisticated and discerning when it comes to gender than many adults.

[38] Spiritual discernment is the same thing as discernment, only applied to religion, spirituality, spiritual concepts, and spiritual thinking.

curriculum on this planet.

Nevertheless, even though you are not taught to discern as a child, you can still easily learn as an adult because it is just not that hard. There are two steps that you can take if you want to learn to discern. **The first step**, raising your expectations *vis a vis* the truth of this world, you have hopefully already taken. **The next step** is to develop a fuller connection with the light of your own higher Self or, as I like to call it, your **Resident Monadic Consciousness**,[39] and that's all. Ideally, you want to raise your expectations, expand your connection to Consciousness, encourage the descent of Consciousness into The Vessel, and rely on your higher self for discernment. You want to do this because you cannot fool your higher Consciousness: you cannot fool God. As stated in *The Book of Light*,[40] Consciousness is awareness pure and simple. Not only that, but Consciousness is the root of all things, and the fundamental ground of all reality. Consciousness is the world. Consciousness is the universe. When Consciousness is present and we are connected, we are (becoming) aware. When we are aware, we are very,

---

[39] Resident Monadic Consciousness is the LP term for your higher Self, or soul if you like. The term emphasises the fact that your soul "takes up residence" in the vehicle that is your body. For more, http://www.thespiritwiki.com/RMC

[40] Michael Sharp, The Book of Light: The Nature of God, the Structure of Consciousness, and the Universe within You, vol. one -air, 4 vols. (St. Albert, Alberta: Lightning Path Press, 2006).

very, very difficult to fool.

I mean, you cannot lie to somebody about your addictions when they are aware the addictions are there. Similarly, you cannot lie to someone about politics, economics, or toxic and abusive situations when people are aware of the problems. For these reasons and more, when it comes to discerning, having more Consciousness in the vessel (i.e. the body) is the surest way to go.

When you have a healthy physical unit and good connection to Consciousness, you have an automatic sensibility and awareness about what is true and false that is right almost all of the time![41]

It is exactly like following your gut/intuition when your gut is connected to God; when that is the case, you know in your gut, in your heart, or in your head when something is just not right about something or somebody, even if you cannot see it with your eyes. Sometimes it is a headache, sometimes you are sick to your stomach, sometimes you get angry, and sometimes you just know. Consciousness is aware of all things and so when Consciousness is present, Consciousness knows. Call this your Internal BS

---

[41] This only sounds crazy if you think Consciousness is somehow limited to the physical vessel in which it manifests. It is not. The vessel is nothing more than a pinprick opening through which Consciousness peers into physical Creation. When you finally realize just how big Consciousness really is you will have no trouble accepting the strong epistemological claims made here.

Detector (IBD) if you like. When it is active, human beings are very, very hard to fool.

Of course, there is a problem with your internal BS detector and that problem is that toxic socialization, toxic parenting, abuse, and lack of proper training has suppressed your **Energy System**,[42] cut off your connection, left you isolated from Consciousness and alone in the darkness. Put another way, the nascent connection to The Fabric of Consciousness that you had as a newborn baby was cut off by the emotional, psychological, physical, sexual, and spiritual violence you have experienced. All this violence has damaged your physical unit, especially the emotional and psychological functionality, and left you disconnected from Consciousness and unnecessarily diminished. Put yet another way, all the abuse you experience within the System shuts down your internal BS detector. This leaves you in a bad position! No internal BS detector means the best way to discern is gone.

So what do you do?

---

[42] Your energy system is basically your body's chakra system. Your chakra system consists of seven main chakras which run down the length of your body from head to the bottom of your torso, and thousands of minor chakra points. For more see http://www.thespiritwiki.com/Energy_System and also Michael Sharp, Dossier of the Ascension: A Practical Guide to Chakra Activation and Kundalini Awakening (Lightning Path Press, 2003).

Well, the best thing to do is to get that internal BS detector back up and running. You can do that by activating chakras, engaging in **Right Thinking**,[43] clearing emotional and psychological blockages, and rebuilding your connection to The Fabric.[44] The problem with this is that it can take a while (a year or two of concerted effort, maybe more) to get energies flowing again. In that time you can remain quite vulnerable to sneaky and sophisticated individuals trying to misdirect, redirect, and/or exploit your nascent interest in awakening and activation. In that vulnerable state, it is easy to confuse you, block you up, and turn you around. Obviously, you want to avoid that. You want to keep moving forward, especially seeing as you have come so far. The question here becomes, what do you do while you are waiting to come back online? If you want to reduce your chance of getting sidetracked or led astray by profits, pundits, and

---

[43] Right thinking, or Right thought, is thought that leads to connection. Right thought is thought that supports Spiritual Awakening. Right thought is thought that supports the expansion of consciousness into the physical unit. For example, the idea that God is a punishing patriarchal God is wrong thought because it leads, as outlined in my *Dossier of the Ascension,* to fear of Connection. Similarly, the idea that we are sinful and unworthy is also wrong thought because it also leads to disconnection.

For more, see http://www.thespiritwiki.com/Right_Thought. For a detailed run down of right and wrong thought, see my *Book of the Triumph of Spirit* series.
http://www.thespiritwiki.com/Book_of_the_Triumph_of_Spirit/.

[44] If you want some guidance on how to do all that, visit http://www.thelightningpath.com/.

gurus of no account, engage some critical sensibility, think carefully about the materials you read, and use what I like to call **Discernment Red Flags**. We shall turn to a discussion of these next.

Discernment Red Flags

The question now is, what are discernment red flags? Discernment red flags are clues or signposts that you can use to assess the quality and veracity of specific **Information Streams**.[45] Put another way, discernment red flags are clues and signposts you can use to tell whether authors, channelers, gurus, authority figures, media pundits, etc. *ad nauseam* are telling you the truth. You can consider discernment red flags as your "awakening and activation" signposts if you like. They are like road signs and they tell you whether an information stream, author, guru, book, or whatever is likely to move you forward, or hold you back. Ask yourself the question, "Does the information stream lead towards awakening and activation or does it lead to disconnection and death?" In the early stages of awakening when the internal **BS** detector is inactive and the blindfold remains firmly in place (or even only partially removed), discernment red flags can help you answer the question, and tell the difference.

As you might expect there is no rocket science here.

---

[45] An *Information Stream* (a.k.a. message stream) is a "channel" of communication between one individual or group and another individual or group. Information streams are everywhere! If you turn on your television you are opening an information stream. If you listen to the radio you are tuned into an information stream. If you listen to rock music, read a book, or listen to a spiritual teacher like me, you are connected to an information stream.

Discernment red flags are straightforward, easy to see (especially after they have been pointed out once), and easy to understand. Still, even though discernment red flags are obvious, you can run into some internal obstacles that make it difficult to see and use these flags. I am speaking here specifically of certain "inner voices" that have been programmed into you in order to prevent you from exercising discernment. The problem will become obvious as you begin your discernment practice, and especially as you start to look critically at spiritual materials. You will be reading a passage or watching a video and you will see one, then two, then three, and maybe even more discernment red flags glaring back at you. The implication, i.e. that the information stream is tainted, corrupted, and disjunctive, will be startling and you may have to admit that some (maybe all) of the information stream you are currently accessing is baloney.

"Wow", you will say to yourself.

"Why didn't I see that before?" you will ask.

It is at exactly this point, or maybe a little before, that the problem will arise. As soon as you see the red flags, as soon as you start to become aware of the BS, as soon as you start to say to yourself "that's not right", a little voice in your head is going to start up and say things like "Don't be so mean", or "Be nice", or "Don't be rude". That little voice is going to say "Don't be so critical" or "Don't be so judgmental", etc. That voice is going to tell you that "all paths lead home" and that

"Everybody is just trying their best". That voice is going to encourage you to accept passively whatever information stream you are accessing no matter how ridiculous it may be.

It is true.

As soon as you start to open your eyes to the truth that some information is just total baloney, that voice is going to chime up and encourage you to accept it anyway. Like some wart-encrusted little gremlin kicking at your shins and scurrying away every time you look to see, that voice will disarm you, distract you, and leave you open to the BS in the information stream. Do not let it do that! If you listen to it, as you might do at first, if you allow yourself to be distracted, you will end up eating baloney, dealing with unnecessary consequences, and slowing yourself down. If you listen to that voice you may even end up bumped off the path. If you want to avoid that eventuality then you must shut that little voice down.

Do not let it speak to you.

Cut it off. Silence it. Push it away. Trust your gut instincts, trust your intellectual awareness of the red flags, and do not let the little demon sow doubt or encourage acceptance. You are not doing anybody any favors if you accept spiritual baloney. Raise your standards and apply them with conviction. *The truth is, not all paths lead home.* Some paths will get you there, some will not. Some will move you forward fast, and some will bog you down. Some will lead you to light, and some will get you addicted to the spiritual equivalent of crack cocaine. If you want to make good forward progress, you are going to have to learn to tell the difference between the two. As I said above, if you cannot be immediately connected with Consciousness, if you cannot immediately rely on your internal BS detector, then you need to keep an eye out for discernment red flags. When you see even one of these red flags, my advice to you is pause and think carefully about the information you are receiving, and be aware of the controlling program inside! As you are considering, do not let the little demon that has been programmed into your head slow you down, turn you around, or drag you back down. If it smells like spiritual BS, it probably is.

We are going to turn our attention to enumerating the discernment red flags in a moment, but before we do that let me just enter a final caveat here. Let me say that the presence of a red flag or two does not immediately invalidate the information stream. People are not perfect and they make mistakes as they follow their process. Even the strongest may stumble and fall and it is inevitable that there will be mistakes. You need to be aware and critical, but you do not need to close your mind totally. If you see a red flag, and especially if you see more than one, be alert, pay closer attention, be discerning, but don't reject the information outright. Observe, process, and think about what you are seeing. Remember, a red flag is not a switch that tells you with certainty that a message stream is bad. It is simply a warning sign that means something may be wrong here, pay critical attention.

With that said it is now time to turn our attention to the discernment red flags. For the purpose of this short monograph, I am going to break discernment red flags down into four broad categories, these being:

1. identity red flags,

2. behavioral red flags,

3. quality of teaching red flags, and

4. ideology red flags.

Briefly, *identity red flags* are flags that point to ego damage and/or ego corruption and may thus indicate forms of mental distortion or illness that may corrupt the stream. *Behavioral red flags* are flags that provide hints on the quality of an individual's connection to The Fabric of Consciousness. *Quality of teaching flags* provide clues on the commitment of the individual to their purpose and mission. Finally, *ideology flags* give indications on the trustworthiness of the individuals teachings based on the presence of self-serving, special interest, ideology. We will look at each of these starting with identity red flags.

DISCERNMENT RED FLAGS - IDENTITY ISSUES

The first red flags we are going to look at are the identity flags. As noted above, identity red flags are red flags that point to ego damage in the physical unit. Without going into too much detail about the psychology behind this, ego damage is a problem in message streams because when an ego is damaged the message stream is often given over to the egoic interests of the individual. If the individual has damaged self-esteem for example, then she or he may use the message stream not to communicate truth but instead to prop up his or her own sense of self-worth. If they do then obviously the message stream becomes less about *your* awakening and activation and more about *their* mental illness. You have to ask yourself the question, if the message stream is not about your awakening and activation, why bother with it at all?

I Channel Famous Dead People

As far as identity red flags go, there are a couple of obvious ones you can look for. One of the surest signs of ego damage, and one of the most obvious identity red flags, is when people start claiming to be representatives of famous dead people. I call this red flag the "*I channel famous dead people*" flag. This flag should be raised and critical discernment engaged whenever you hear some spiritual author, guru, channeler, or avatar wannabe try and tell you how they work with this famous dead person or that famous dead person, or if one famous dead person isn't enough, this or that group of famous dead people. It can actually border on the absurd at times. I had one fellow who approached me once who literally channeled the entire "galactic hierarchy". All the Elohim, all the "special creator aspects" of God, all the various "Galactic Councils of Light" and just about every famous prophet East, West, North, and South were coming through this guy, or so he said. It was cosmic name-dropping to the nth degree and it was absurd to the nth degree. And he's not the only example! Here is another taken from some random web page of a "spiritually awakened" woman channeling back in 2010. Notice that she does not appear to be concerned with your spiritual awakening at all! Her primary desire here seems to be to convey to us how special she really is.

> I have been trained by C. to speak 'Energy Verbs of Fresh Creation', as super high and quick frequencies are transmitted through me. I am working together with the Angels on High, the best aspects of God, all the high level Galactic Councils of Light, all the most significant Ascended White Guys, and everybody else that you might recognize as important to bring this super fundamental work forward as part of the highest level Divine Plan.

I have paraphrased the words a bit to protect the

identity of this poor, lost soul, so you won't find this exact text on the Internet. However, you will find many texts just like it. Notice how she has been "specially trained", how she speaks with "very fast frequencies", and how she works with all sorts of very famous, very powerful, and very important dead guys (and it is usually guys). These are huge red flags. These sorts of "listen to me/love me because I'm so special and connected" statements are the sign of desperate need for love and attention and a very damaged bodily ego. The reality is that whoever it is that is issuing these claims does not feel good about themselves at all. This individual has no confidence in her own abilities and expertise. She does not believe that she can be loved and accepted on her own merit. In order to get love, she feels she must be anybody else but herself. Her self-esteem has been destroyed, almost certainly by her parents and teachers, and in order to bolster her shattered sense of self she issues statements and fantasizes connection to spirits that make her feel special and important and good about herself.

Of course, it is bad enough that these red flags indicate a person lost in mental anguish and suffering. It is worse when we consider the fact that an individual in this psychological state is very susceptible to **Temptation**[46] and therefore highly prone to

---

[46] Temptation is anything that turns the physical unit away from connection. Temptation is anything that interferes with alignment or that causes disjuncture. People give in to

Communication Errors.[47] And when I say "highly susceptible" I really mean inevitably susceptible.

Individuals with low self-esteem will invariably insert errors and corruptions into an information stream as they attempt to fill the gaping holes left in their damaged psyches by the toxic socialization process they endured.

The basic dynamic is simple and arises because of fractured attachment, destroyed self-esteem, and chronically experienced conditional love. An adult with fractured attachments and low self-esteem, an adult who has been raised with the feeling that they will only be loved when they perform adequately,[48] has an often desperate need to secure positive regard (i.e. love) from others by showing how well they perform! Because **unmet egoic needs are powerful and pre-**

---

temptation not because they are evil but because they are needy, sick, and unconscious. People give into temptation in an effort to fulfill unmet needs, soothe damaged wounds, distract themselves from difficult realities, and for other pathological reasons. Note, often, predators exploit temptation in order to gain control of an individual physical unit.
http://www.thespiritwiki.com/Temptation

[47] A Communication Error is an error in a message stream caused by a systemic problem with the information source. The presence of communication errors *invalidates* an individual message and even the entire message stream. See www.thespiritwiki.com/Communication_Error

[48] That is, get a good grade at school, get a home run at the ball game, dress real pretty and proper, be a compliant little "show piece" for the family, etc.

emptive motivators, the physical unit is driven to fulfil these needs. In situations like this, information accuracy and spiritual responsibility take a back seat to the desperate need to prop up damaged self-esteem and gain external attention. In their attempts to satisfy unmet psychological and emotional needs, they (and by "they" I mean channelers, reporters, actors, writers, and anyone else involved in the communication of message and meaning) will do and say just about anything that they think will please others and win them the love, approval, and positive regard that they so desperately require. In this process, communications become self-serving and truth is sacrificed at the altar of human psychopathology.

I realize this may be a bit abstract at this point, but perhaps an example or two will help. Imagine that I want to talk to you about spiritual things but because of the toxic socialization of my childhood, I now have damaged self-esteem. In this situation, powerful and unmet needs shape my communications with you. In this situation, I will talk to you and tell you things not because I want to uplift you (though that may be what I tell you) but because I am driven to satisfy my ego needs in a desperate attempt to heal my damaged psyche. For example, the truth might be that if you want to advance spiritually, if you want awaken, activate, and ascend, you have to bring your physical unit into **Alignment**[49] with your **Resident Monadic Self (RMS)**[50] (a.k.a. your Resident Monadic Consciousness or your "higher" self). The truth might be that in order to be in alignment with your RMS you have to stop hurting, exploiting, and killing others period, no excuses. The truth might be that if you do not stop your "evil ways" right now you will continue to drive a wedge between your bodily ego and your RMS. The truth might be that if you continue to drive a wedge between your bodily ego and your RMS you will begin (if you have not already) to experience the anxiety, guilt and shame of *disjuncture*. The truth might be that you won't want to experience those feelings because they are so very, very painful. The truth might be that in order to avoid the ugly feelings of disjuncture you may *turn away* from people who utter these truths and "settle" for lower consciousness, eventually going to your grave without experiencing true connection to

---

[49] Alignment is a concept that refers, generally, to the state of the physical reality as a reflection of Consciousness. When physical reality accurately reflects the will, intent, and desires of Consciousness we may say that physical creation is in alignment with Consciousness. When physical reality does not reflect the will, intent, and desire of Consciousness we may say that physical creation is out of alignment.

Alignment may also refer, more specifically, to the extent to which your physical vehicle is aligned with its own higher Consciousness. See http://twww.thespiritwiki.com/Alignment

[50] Resident Monadic Self (RMS) is another term for Resident Monadic Consciousness, or Consciousness as it inhabits the physical body. Use the term RMS when you wish to emphasize the *identity/ego* aspects of instantiated Consciousness. See http:// www.thespiritwiki.com/RMC

higher Consciousness. Therefore, the truth might be that if you are serious about spiritual awakening and connection you have to *smarten up this instant.*

What can I say?

The truth might be a bitter pill to swallow, but you may never get to swallow it because the truth is very, very, very few spiritual teachers are going to tell you the truth because most are more concerned with their own damaged egos than they are with your spiritual progress. The truth is, telling you these truths is a straight up risk for them. The truth is they may be desperate for your attention. The truth is if they tell you these truths, they risk your disapproval and rejection. The truth is, upon hearing/reading these hard truths you may become defensive, offended, or even triggered; as a result, you may withhold your attention and turn away.

You can see the problem.

If my goal is your awakening and empowerment, I will say these truths no matter what you do or what you think. I will tell you these things even if I think you might walk away because I know you need to hear them. On the other hand, if my goal is selfish then I will not tell you what you need to hear. If my motivation is egoic, I will not tell you the truth because I will be afraid to lose you as a "fan". If my motivation is egoic, I am not going to say anything or do anything that I think is going to make you not like me. If my motivation is egoic, if I am trying to assuage damaged self-esteem or reassemble shattered ego, my goal is your approval. In order to win that approval I am going to do and say anything I must. Thus, instead of telling you the truth, the whole truth, and nothing but the truth no compromise and no strings attached I will tell you what will entertain you, draw your attention, and make you love me. I may avoid making certain statements, I may sugarcoat the statements I do make, and I may even outright lie to you to protect my emotional, psychological, and even financial interests.

For example, maybe in order to avoid offending all the rich people in the world I'll tell you that greed and obscene wealth in the face of global poverty (read "austerity") and child starvation is part of the "checkerboard" plan of creation and therefore not your problem. Maybe, in order to avoid offending all the people who use violence to get their way I will tell you that anger, hatred, and violence is sourced in God's will to judge and punish, and therefore OK in the grander scheme. Maybe, in order to make it look easier than it really is, I will tell you that all you have to do is tap, tap, tap or rub, rub, rub some crystals and everything will be OK. Maybe I will tell you a lot of things to protect my interests, but whatever I say doesn't really matter here. What matters here is that you recognize just how serious a problem this is! If my motivation is egoic, I will say just about anything I think will get your attention and make you like me. I just do not care about anything else. Once I make my ego the goal of my teaching I have totally undermined the message stream and totally sacrificed your spiritual progress in the interest of my ego gratification. This is obviously a major problem for you, especially if you are concerned with authentic spiritual knowledge and practice. Therefore, if you see people channeling famous or powerful dead people, if you hear them uttering "listen to me/love me" statements that seem designed to attract you and lock in your attention, ask yourself the hard question. *Are you prepared to put your spiritual health, the health of your family and children, and the health of this planet, in the hands of an individual or individuals whose primary motivation is egoic?* If not, tread carefully whenever you see this particular discernment red flag.

I AM a Famous Dead Person

It is bad enough when people claim to be channeling famous dead people; however, the red flag becomes a veritable alarm bell when a channeler does not just claim to channel famous dead people, they claim to actually be famous dead people. In this case, the ego damage may be so dramatic, the self-esteem so thoroughly crushed and destroyed, and the self-loathing so pronounced and uncontrollable, that this person has to actually be someone else in order to feel good about themselves. In this case all the caveats stated above under the "I channel famous dead people" red flag apply, but with a multiplication factor of about one hundred.

Any truth you get from a person who is so pathologically unsatisfied with their own self that they have to claim to be someone else will be so full of ego-juice as to be indistinguishable from nonsense.

This is a strong statement I know, but in the swirling energies of end-times transformation, the last thing you want to do is to get caught up behind some ego-damaged blindfolded person as they struggle and thrash in the foam and chop of their own ego serving delusions.[51] My advice to you, take it or leave it, is simple. If you find somebody claiming to be this famous dead person or that famous dead prophet, run. While it is true that they may be connected, and while it is true that they may even have a strong channel open, the information that comes through their stream may end up so corrupted and distorted as to be useless at best, and misleading, deceiving, and damaging to your own health and well-being at worst. If you see people claiming to be something they are clearly not, fly the red flag.

---

[51] Besides, as you should understand at this point, we are not doing anybody any favours when we sugar coat the truth. When we sugar coat we fail to convey important information, like serious urgency or profound danger. When we sugar coat information we harm the people we are trying to save by enabling their delusions and dysfunctions. This is especially true in times of crises. If you want to help others and not just yourself, be real at all times.

DISCERNMENT RED FLAGS –
BEHAVIORAL/ALIGNMENT ISSUES

Now of course, not all spiritual gurus, world teachers, or "avatar" wannabes claim to be channels. Some people support their claim to spiritual expertise on the strength of their own actions and words. The problem is, sometimes actions and words are out of alignment with one's own RMC. In these cases, we say that an individual has, in relation to the desires and expectations of their RMC, behavioral issues. Behavioral issues are a critical red flag because these issues point to poor connection to The Fabric. The truth is, *individuals with a strong connection to The Fabric will act "in alignment" with their own RMC.* If an individual is not acting in alignment, you need to question their connection, knowledge, and even motivation.

Identifying individuals with behavioral issues, identifying individuals who act out of alignment, can be a little harder than identifying someone with identity issues. To identify behavioural/alignment issues, you have to do your due diligence, and one of the things you can research is their current behavior. You have no doubt heard the aphorism actions speak louder than words. This is certainly true, and this adage applies to spiritual teachers, gurus and avatars more than anyone else. If you want to judge somebody's character, if you want to judge the true strength of their connection to The Fabric, judge it by their actions because actions speak louder than words. If their behaviours are good and their actions aligned, chances are good they have a decent connection to consciousness. If there actions are not aligned, then question the veracity of their claims. The question now becomes, what sorts of actions will we be looking for?

Well, because of the **Nature of Consciousness**,[52] someone who has a strong connection to The Fabric will be moral, ethical, just, and fair. Someone with a strong connection to The Fabric will also be devoid of chronic anger, hatred, excuse, and abuse and will (despite the very toxic world we live in) act this way most, if not all, of the time. By contrast, someone who is not so strongly connected to The Fabric will have neither the foundation nor the structure for ethical and aligned action. As a result, they will very often *not* act in a moral, ethical, just, nonviolent and loving manner,

---

[52] The nature of consciousness refers to the inherent character of Consciousness, specifically as that character emerges from the fundamental facets and aspects of Consciousness. The nature of a car is that it is a vehicle of transportation. This purpose, coupled with the fact it has wheels, is made of metal, and responds to the intent of the driver, defines its nature. Because of its nature, which is determined by the elements of its construction and the purpose of its creation, you use a car to drive and not hammer nails. The nature of consciousness is that it is blissful, awareness, powerful, loving, and imaginative. For reasons outlined elsewhere, consciousness can no more be ignorant, angry, impotent, hateful, and dull as a car could be an implement used to hammer a small nail. For more on the nature of Consciousness see Sharp, The Book of Light: The Nature of God, the Structure of Consciousness, and the Universe within You.

despite their claims to be connected.

Of course, as noted above, people without connection can claim to be wise, wonderful, and spiritual, but words are energetically cheap. You do not burn any calories at all by lying about the kind of person you are. On the other hand, actions take work and energy. If you know where people put most of their energy, if you know how they act, then like magic you know what their priorities and values are. If they are acting with greed, anger, hatred, violence, arrogance, and abuse, then my advice is, question their connection.

Watching where people spend their energy in order to determine what their values and priorities are works for everybody, but it is particularly important when it comes to those individuals who claim the **Mantle of Spiritual Authority**.[53] People who don the mantle of spiritual authority are people who are speaking with authority about things of a spiritual nature. These people (and I am one of them) generally will claim a strong relationship to God and a powerful and pure

---

[53] The Mantle of Spiritual Authority (or just The Mantle or MASA for short) is a (usually metaphoric) garment that an individual dons when they presume to speak the capital "T" truths of Consciousness, God, and creation. The mantle of spiritual authority is like the red robe that a priest uses to distinguish himself from the congregation. It is a claim of authority and wisdom designed to indicate spiritual and pedagogical mastery. The individual who dons The Mantle presumes to speak spiritual truths, and pedagogical mastery because the wearer presumes to be a good teacher. For more, see http://www.thespiritwiki.com/The_Mantle/.

connection to Consciousness. The thing to remember here is that connection to Consciousness necessarily leads to increased alignment. You can thus expect that someone who is connected to will behave in an aligned fashion. Nobody is perfect of course and "even" Jesus got angry off from time to time, but the general tone and tenor of behavior should always be towards increasingly aligned existence. The bottom line is simple. *If I (or anybody else) claim high connection to God, then my behaviors should be generally (and increasingly) aligned with higher Consciousness.* If not, then I am not as connected and wise as I claim to be, and hence probably a waste of time to listen to. This goes for any priest, prophet, guru, evangelist, or whatever. If the individual claiming connection does not walk the walk, do not follow them. Instead, fly the red flag. Remember, we all have a limited amount of time and energy to play with. If we want to make the most progress forward, we need to be careful where we spend our energy.

Don't be an A-hole

Speaking of paying attention to people's actions, the first behavioral red flag we can look at in this category is "a-hole behavior". This red flag works out simple and is easy to understand. If, for example, God is love and Allah is kind and merciful then people who claim to speak in "the name of" must not be a-holes. They must be loving and kind, merciful and fair. If they are not, if they are violent, judgmental, mean, hurtful, greedy, selfish, and cold, then they probably aren't speaking for the one they claim to be speaking for!

I'm just saying...

People, who are authentically connected to The Fabric of Consciousness, people who are in touch with the higher truths of creation, people who are in tune with their own divinity (and the divinity of others), do not act like a-holes. People who are connected to their compassionate and loving monadic self display compassion, love, and empathy in all things. They are not mean and vindictive; they do not abuse and exploit; they do not lie and dissemble. And note, this is not necessarily because they are acting out of some intellectual or moral sensibility but because they are authentically connected, necessarily aligned, clearly aware, and strongly identified with the divinity that lies within all of us. People who are truly connected do not display the same disjunctive behaviors as people who are disconnected.

If you want to evaluate a candidate for your attention, look for equality, justice, love, compassion, and mercy not only in their teachings, but also (and especially) in their actions.

Look to see if they treat their employees with respect; look to see if they protect, nurture, and spend time with their children; look to see if they are supportive and helpful; look to see if they are aware of reality; look to see if they fight for injustice. In short, look to see if they represent Consciousness. If they do not, if you find them in the service of inequality, injustice, hatred, and so on, walk swiftly away.

Of course, having said this, a couple of caveats are in order. **The first caveat,** remember, we are all in human form. Each one of you reading this word is in a human body, and human bodies are mere flesh and blood. Because of the nature of the body, because of the weaknesses of the flesh, because of the programming of the body, and because of the vile social and economic condition of this world, we all make mistakes. We all get frustrated; we all get angry; we all get hurt; we all get violent; we all screw up. That is OK. Nobody in the cosmos, least of all God, is worried if you mess up, especially while in body. It is the nature of blindfolded physical manifestation. While in body, while incarnated in a blindfolded physical unit, while living in the vile and toxic conditions of this planet, we all make mistakes. None of us is perfect even when strongly connected and so we need to cut people a little slack. Even saints make mistakes. The difference to look for is *those who are connected will own up, take responsibility, quickly atone,* and *strive for better behavior.* An individual locked in the destructive embrace of a damaged and disconnected ego will deny, deny, deny and avoid, avoid, avoid. If someone makes mistakes, cut them some slack. However if they deny their mistakes, if they try to make their behavior look like a good thing when clearly it isn't, and if they otherwise avoid facing the negative reality of their own actions, they are probably not as connected as they may want you to think, or as they think they are. A person who assaults and controls women (or men), a person who steals and exploits, a person who manipulates and deceives, cannot be trusted to deliver truth, especially if they deny responsibility and accountability. A mistake or two here and there is OK if there is responsibility and accountability, but walk if the red flags are flying!

The second caveat I want to enter concerning actions that are out of alignment is this; *being loving and compassionate towards others does not mean enabling bad behavior.* Some spiritual people, especially those of the "new age" variety, will tell you that the only person you are responsible for is yourself and therefore you should just let everyone else do their own thing. Unfortunately for them, that is simply not true, and it is not true for a couple of reasons. **First of all**, it is not true because actions have wide impact. What I do with my body and my life affects others. The food I choose to eat, the addictions I choose to serve, the way I treat my kids, the way I treat my colleagues, etc., all matters. If I abuse a admin assistant at work and that admin assistant then goes home to abuse their children, *I AM RESPONSIBLE,* and I mean in a moral, ethical, and karmic sense. If I see a coworker abusing an admin assistant and I do not say or do anything about it, *I AM RESPONSIBLE.* Therefore I must always act (sensibly, within reason, and with consideration for both making it worse and my own personal safety) to reduce negativity, toxicity, and disjuncture. It is the way it is. You are not loving someone when you let them smoke, drink to excess, do drugs, hurt their children, or harm others (even if they are harming others in another country). When you do that, you are enabling not supporting and participating in their self-destruction.

The second reason that it is not true that you are only responsible for yourself is simply because you are a spark of divine Consciousness incarnated. You are a spark of God Consciousness incarnated in a physical unit and as such, you are the **Hand of The Fabric**.[54] In other words, you are the one that gets things done "down here" in **The World**.[55] Therefore, you have a responsibility to challenge, take control, and change things. If your husband is a sexist patriarch, if your brother is an alcoholic, if your sister is exploiting and abusing her employees, do not smile and wave and do not "maintain your bliss" by remaining ignorant! **Say something; do something; act**. Remember, being compassionate does not mean you must enable other's

---

[54] The Hand of the Fabric (a.k.a. Hand of God) is a phrase used to emphasize the fact that the individual monad incarnated in a physical body is an important "implement" by which the intention and desires of Consciousness become implemented in reality. Thus we might say then when you are connected and fully aligned, you become a Hand of the Fabric. http://www.thespiritwiki.com/Hand_of_the_Fabric/.

[55] The World is a New Energy Archetype in Michael Sharp's New Energy Halo/Sharp archetype deck. The World archetype refers to physical reality. See http://www.thespiritwiki.com/The_World/.

abuse and toxicity. In fact, it means exactly the opposite. When you love someone, you do not allow him or her to engage in self-destructive behaviors. You cannot chain people down of course, but you can draw boundaries and set expectations. Do not drink alcohol around your alcoholic brother; demand your abusive husband enter into family therapy; tell your sister to stop abusing her employees, etc. In short, be authentically compassionate and supportive by being strong and saying no, nada, and no way.

Of course, since we are talking about discernment here, look for this in the words and works of others as well. If a guru or priest or prophet is advising you to ignore and allow bad behavior (by telling you to turn your attention away, telling you that people must find their own way, telling you that it is all about "free will", or offering you sound bites about "cosmic freedom") be wary and ask the hard question.[56] It is true that you

---

[56] I have a great example of this. Years ago, I remember listening to a channelled communication from some U.S. based channeler. The channellers were advising parents to avoid "getting in the way" of the child's inner divinity. In practice, this meant, among other things, allowing the child to have a computer in their bedroom and not "policing" their internet time. When I heard this, I was horrified. Were these individuals not aware of the rampant child abuse? Did they not know that predators lurk the Internet looking for unattended children? Did they not understand their role as parents was to nurture and protect? I asked the hard questions and when I told my wife, she asked an even harder question. She simply asked, were these people paedophiles? Unfortunately, we had to answer maybe. Perhaps they were reaching out through the nascent

cannot change people who do not want to change; however, it also true that you do not have to support, spend time with, listen to, or otherwise enable people locked in disconnection and pathology. Do not go down with their sinking ship. Fly the red flag and save yourself.[57] It is okay to love someone while not loving their behavior. You can confront them with love in your heart. The truth may hurt; however, this is the hurt associated with treating a wound, not the hurt associated with assault and damage. Remember this: We all deserve the truth; we all need the truth; we will all recover only when surround by the truth, the whole truth, and nothing but the truth.

Internet to create a world where they could have sex with people's kids. It sounds outrageous but *the reality is paedophiles* are well organized, technologically sophisticated, and active predators. Theirs are not crimes of opportunity but of premeditation. There is a reason they call it "grooming" and we had to wonder, were these people grooming parents and their children so that the parents would leave the child unattended, unsupervised, and accessible? Seems outrageous at first glance, but as the highly organized nature of global paedophile networks comes increasingly to light, it is not unreasonable to suggest.

[57] If this sounds a bit selfish, let me explain. If you are on a boat with your family or friends and suddenly that boat sinks, plunging you and your entire group into the cold waters, the best thing you can do is make sure you are safe before you try and help others. This is especially true if you are not a strong swimmer to begin with. A drowning adult can take down even the strongest swimmer. Even lifeguards have to be careful. If you and the people around you are drowning, *get to a position of safety and strength first,* and then reach out to help. Of course if there is a child in the water, save that child as you save yourself; but, if you are dealing with other strong adults, save yourself first.

Hierarchical Tendencies

In addition to looking broadly at behavioral red flags, in particular a-hole behavior, you can also look for the red flag of hierarchy. By hierarchy, I simply mean the rank ordering of people into levels of worth where some people are said to be worth more and deserve more than others who are said to be worth less and deserve less. If you see a spiritual teacher justifying (or worse participating in) hierarchy, *run in the opposite* direction because the presence of hierarchy is a sure sign that something is amiss. The truth is, there is no hierarchy in heaven and no justification for it on Earth. As I explain in *The Book of Light: The Nature of God, the Structure of Consciousness, and the Universe Within You*, we are all equal co-creative sparks in the glorious Fabric of Consciousness. *In the eyes of Consciousness and Spirit, all beings are equal and equally deserving.* As such, there is no room for hierarchy or exclusion Failure to understand and represent this truth in word and deed is a dead giveaway of disconnection, disjuncture, lack of understanding, deliberate obfuscation, or self-serving justifications for power and greed.

Now, this all seems simple enough and reasonable to anybody who understands the true nature of Consciousness. Nevertheless and despite the deep egalitarian nature of consciousness, you will find that many so-called gurus and teachers, especially quite successful ones, import the hierarchical and exclusionary thinking of the old paradigms into their writing, even if they start out with right thinking! It often comes down to their own failure to resist *temptation*, the subsequent need to justify the power and privilege they may accrue, and desire to assuage their guilt and shame at having giving in and (essentially) giving up.

Consider this story. I visited South Africa a few years ago and at a gathering one night, I was expected to sit in what, for all intents and purposes, was a throne. The hostess of the evening setup the throne and arranged in typical fashion, at the head and center of the room. It was very flattering that she thought I deserved this special treatment, but all I saw was the authority, hierarchy, and privilege that this represented. I turned her down and made her husband sit in the throne instead. She was not impressed and would not speak to me after that. She felt I had personally insulted her by refusing to be glorified and exalted above all others in the room. It really was not about her, it was about staying aligned by actively representing the truth that we all deserve the same levels of respect, regard, and reward regardless of race, class, status, gender, or whatever. The point, we are all equal and deserving in the eyes of Consciousness, God, Krishna, Allah, etc. and nobody, not even me, deserves to be singled out and given special treatment. I stood by the truth and that offended her.

Of course, things could have gone a different way. If my ego had been damaged, if my self-esteem was not sufficient, if I had unmet needs from childhood, I may have decided to sit on the throne provided. Giving into the **Ego Temptation,**[58] I may have welcomed the adulation and respect. If I had sat in that chair, if I had agreed to participate in the game of hierarchy being played that night, if I had started down that road, not only would it become easier and easier for me to give in to the old energies, but I would have eventually found it necessary to justify my weakness by modifying what I teach in order to support the hierarchy and privilege that I had given in to. I cannot tell you that there is no hierarchy in heaven and then go on to embrace it here on Earth, can I? If I did not want to look like a total hypocrite, I would have to start saying something different. Perhaps instead of suggesting we are all equal in the eyes of God, I would tell my readers and myself that it is right to exalt the wise teacher because he is a special emissary,[59] even when it is not.

---

[58] An ego temptation is basically anything that "feeds" an ego. Ego temptations include things like power, wealth, toxic sexuality, attention, privilege over others, etc. Ego temptations "feed" a bodily ego. Although there is nothing wrong with "feeding" a bodily ego, it can become a problem when the ego is damaged and/or The System exploits ego needs in order to support its own operation. www.thespiritwiki.com/Ego_Temptation/.

[59] Note, "exalting" someone in a hierarchy is different than recognizing somebody for their expertise and/or achievements. We all need positive reinforcement, love, respect, and attention and we should give this out more freely than we do. What we do not need is to couple that recognition and attention with notions of worth, privilege, hierarchy, authority, and differential reward. We all have our strengths and accomplishments. These can be recognized and we can accept these without participating in the vile hierarchies of the old energy world.

Perhaps I would say that God in the Heaven sits on a throne and that makes it OK for me to sit on a throne as well. Perhaps I would say that it is a "natural" expression of the "natural order" of things. Perhaps I would say that the throne is a sign of strength and superiority and *not* of a damaged ego. I could say many things, but the details are not important. What is important is that we recognize that when we see somebody give in to ego temptations, when we see them embrace hierarchy and privilege, when we see them, in other words, sit down on a throne, we should fly the red flag and ask the hard questions. Are they really connected to The Fabric and can they really understand the nature of Reality, or have they given in to ego temptation? If they have given in to temptation, are they compromising their teachings and sacrificing the truth in order to justify and excuse their mistakes, weaknesses, or sicknesses? If you think they are compromising the truth in order to justify their mistakes, weakness, or sickness, walk away. You will have a hard time connecting yourself to Consciousness if you do not clear out ideas that support hierarchy and exclusion. Frankly, you will have a hard time clearing out ideas that support hierarchy and exclusion if you are constantly feeding these ideas to your brain. Remember the programming adage: garbage in, garbage out. If you want to awaken, activate, and ascend, avoid filling your brain with the disjunctive garbage of hierarchy and privilege.

Hypocrisy and Avoidance of Responsibility

Another broadly behavioral red flag that you should watch out for is avoidance of responsibility. Authentic spiritual teachers, in fact authentic professionals of all stripes, take responsibility seriously. Authentic professionals pay attention to the quality of their work, its reliability and validity, its accuracy, and its impact on others. Put another way, professionals do not just spew anything they want without careful consideration. Professionals take care and are concerned for the wellbeing of those impacted by their work. Inauthentic spiritual teachers, naïve spiritual teachers, disconnected spiritual teachers, teachers who do it for ego or for money, do not care and avoid responsibility.

Now, it might sound like common sense to some, but you do find avoidance of responsibility a lot amongst those who profess to be spiritual authorities. Some young male or female has some kind of "connection experience" and suddenly they are channeling famous and powerful spiritual entities and providing all sorts of psychological, emotional, and spiritual advice. They say, "Do this" and "Do that". They say "This is the truth" and "That is a lie". They give all sorts of advice and guidance, which is fine; but then, they do not follow their own advice, and they do not take their own guidance, and they avoid responsibility for what they say.

I know it sounds a little strange, but it is a problem. Often we find gurus, spiritual teachers, and other purveyors of "spiritual truth" uttering all sorts of crazy things, and then backing away from responsibility by telling you, often explicitly, that they are not responsible for what they are saying. They say, "Use your discernment and decide for yourself because all truths are relative and all paths lead home". And while it is true that you should use your discernment, it is not cool that a teacher should absolve themselves of commitment and responsibility by not standing behind their words and their work. People who distance themselves from their own truths do not have faith in their own utterances, and if that is the case then you have to ask the hard questions. If they do not have faith in what they say, why should you? Trust people that are confident in what they say and that stand by their words and work. Do not trust those who do not. Ask the hard questions about the ones who make strong claims, but then offers disclaimers and avoidance.

This is common sense really. If a carpenter, bridge builder, spiritual teacher, etc. does not have any confidence in their own work, if they tell you up front that they cannot guarantee the quality, or if they say one thing but do another, why on Earth would you hire them? It is hard enough getting proper spiritual bearings in this increasingly lunatic world without wasting time on an individual with no faith even in themselves.

If you want to make good forward progress, you need to be selective about the information streams you tap into.

Remember, "garbage in, garbage out". If a spiritual teacher does not have confidence in, nor do they stand behind the words they say, fly the red flag and ask the hard questions. Can you trust the purveyances of a vendor without confidence, or who does not follow their own good advice? If you answer no, walk away.

One final comment here: if you, the person reading this, are one of those people who teach spiritual things but absolve yourself of responsibility for the things you teach, think about this. If you put out spiritual information and this spiritual information harms others, you are responsible for the harm you inadvertently cause. Whether you like it or not your higher self, your cosmic monad, the big "I" that is the source of the reflected little "i" of your body, will not let you walk away. You do not get to "wash your hands" of your own ill-conceived activity. It is just like if you are a doctor and you prescribe a pill that kills someone, or if you are a bridge engineer who fails to take the time needed to build a safe bridge. If people become ill or die as a result of your actions, you are responsible. If you are uncomfortable with that, uncomfortable with the karmic implications,[60] and do not want to take the time to ensure that the advice you are giving is good

---

[60] Karma is simply the adult action that arises from basic adult responsibility. If you spill a bottle of milk, karmic action is the action you take to clean up your own mess. http://www.thespiritwiki.com/Karma/.

advice, do the responsible thing and do not give advice. My advice to you is, stay silent until you are a) sure you understand and b) confident enough to stand behind the things that you say.

I Have the Magic Wand

Besides lack of confidence, lack of responsibility, the importation of hierarchy, and a-hole behaviour, if you want to discern the wheat from the chaff, you also have to look for outrageous claims. It seems unnecessary to say, however there are people who claim to have some sort of magical wand, magical crystal, or magical ability to heal you, awaken you, activate you, and ascend you with no difficulty at all, and no work on your part. It may be a lightshow, a machine, a crystal, a thumb touch, or even a "real" magic wand. Whatever it is you should know, there are no magic tricks or potions that will cause you to suddenly heal, awaken, and ascend. As explained in the *Book of Light Volume One*,[61] the physical universe, the 3D world, has inertia and it takes time, effort, and faith (in your own ability, and faith in the world around you) to overcome that inertia. Anyone that says differently is selling you snake-oil. This is your journey. The most others can do is assist you with knowledge and incite you toward your awakening, activation, and ascension. If anyone offers to magically heal you, and/or otherwise take that

---

[61] Sharp, <u>The Book of Light: The Nature of God, the Structure of Consciousness, and the Universe within You</u>.

responsibility away from you, do not even bother with the hard questions, simply run in the opposite direction. If you do not do it, if you do not take action, if you do not heal your wounds, read the words, improve your eating habits, fix your environment, do the chakra visualizations, and connect your soul, it ain't happen. It just does not work that way. All you can expect from others is a little physical or energetic support; that is all. If you do not take action, nothing is going to change.

Money's the Motive

Besides looking for lack of confidence, lack of responsibility, hierarchy, a-hole behavior, and claims to have the magic wand, another red flag filed under the behavioral issues category is motivation, in particular the motivation of money. I have to say that it is always the case that when money is the motive, problems ensue.

Now do not get me wrong here, I have nothing at all against money. We all have to eat and we all deserve fair exchange for the work that we do.[62] Indeed, everybody on this Earth deserves to live comfortably, but at some point, a person can become too concerned with money, even when they have much more than enough. Becoming overly concerned with money is

---

[62] For my position on money see Sharp, The Rocket Scientists' Guide to Money and the Economy: Accumulation and Debt.

bad for spiritual truth and an issue for discernment because when money becomes the primary concern, other goals and priorities, like for example spiritual awakening, take a back seat. This is true whether you are an individual who puts aside awakening and ascension because you feel power and money are more important goals to pursue, and it is true if you are a writer writing about spiritual things. When money becomes the goal, truth takes a hit.

I can use myself as an example here. Consider the writing process and the goal of writing. Typically when I write a sentence I judge the sentence, paragraph, book that emerges based on whether or not I feel the sentence, paragraph, book, and corpus is grounded, accessible, TRUE, and effective, with an emphasis on effective. My goal is your awakening, activation, and ascension and as long as I think that a sentence, paragraph, or book effectively contributes to that goal, I am happy. If the sentence, paragraph, or book is off in some way, if I think something else has gotten in (like my own ego, for example), or if I think it is not clear and grounded, I rewrite. My reference point is always a) the statement's contribution to your awakening and activation and b) its ability to communicate to you. If I think a sentence does not align with the reference, I rewrite.

Now imagine that I change my motivation from helping you awaken to taking your money. If my motivation is getting my hands on your money then my primary concern is not with truth and communication, but with saying things to make money. When money is my motive, my reference will be different. When money is my motive, I will think about a sentence, a paragraph, or a book in relation to its ability to get your money. Thus, when money is the motive, I write not to awaken and activate, but to manipulate you for your money. I am sure you will agree, this is a very different reference point.

When money is the motive and the reference is the sale, subtle corruptions enter into the information stream.

If I write a sentence and I think that sentence won't sell, perhaps because I believe the truth will offend you, or perhaps because I think some book critic won't like it, then perhaps I would rewrite the sentence so that the offending truth is not there! In this way, I improve my chances of pleasing the critics and making the money, but I have lowered your chance of awakening and activation because I have taken out a truth that you need to hear. I will not say what you need to hear because I think you will not like it, or will not pay for it. If my goal is manipulating/pleasing you to get your money, I will say totally different things. The point is if my goal is money (or ego, or attention, or anything other than helping you), I will not care about your spiritual progress, I will only care if you like what I say enough to give me your money. And that is a bad thing because it means compromise and corruption throughout. If my reference point is money, I will compromise the truth just to increase my chance of profit. In so doing I sacrifice your awakening and activation on Mammon's foul altar. If you are happy about being sacrificed in that way, fine. If not, discern and be sure. *If you think a prophet is about the profit, fly the red flag.*

DISCERNMENT RED FLAGS - QUALITY OF TEACHING

So far, in this chapter we have discussed behavioral red flags and identity red flags. In addition to these, a third category of red flag is pedagogical, and when I say pedagogical, I am referring to the quality of the teaching. To be blunt, there has to be a certain minimum level of quality to a set of teachings, otherwise it is a red flag. The fact is that Spiritual teachers (a.k.a. gurus, avatars, or whatever you want to call them) essentially come as **World Teachers.**[68] Spiritual teachers come to teach the world, or some part of it, important spiritual truths. Teaching the world is their mission and as such, it is an absolute bare minimum that their teachings be sensible, grounded, logical, intuitive, and effective, otherwise they are violating the parameters of their mission, or they are not on a mission to begin with. Put another way, a

---

[68] A World Teacher is a teacher that incarnates to assist with the awakening, activation, and ascension of a people. See http://www.thespiritwiki.com/World_Teacher

spiritual teacher must be able to teach. If they cannot teach, if their teachings are confused, if your contact with a spiritual teacher leaves you scratching your head or spinning in circles of confusion, then there is a serious problem. If an individual claims to be a teacher but teaches nothing, ask the hard questions.

Just how can you tell if a teacher cannot teach? In order to judge the quality of a teacher you have to look at the content, the students, the goals, and so on. That can be complex for a beginning student to assess, especially when they do not know the content, but it comes down to this. If a teacher teaches a teaching and if most students learn something from the teaching, then it is a quality teaching. On the other hand, if the teacher teaches a teaching and only a few students get it, or if the students walk out more confused than before, then it is not a quality teaching.

This sounds straight forward, right? Unfortunately, it is not as easy as you might think. In order to draw attention away from the poor quality of many spiritual teachings, we (and by "we" I mean all the people of this Earth) have been conditioned to accept disorientation and even confusion as a necessary part of our spiritual training. Many of us accept without question the fact that learning spiritual things is hard. Many of us expect that we should work hard, struggle mightily, and cross many lifetimes to elevate our spiritual game. Many of us expect the teachings to be a major challenge. Do not get me wrong here, following a spiritual path does come with its challenges, but one of those challenges should not be the spiritual teachings. If a person claims to be a world teacher, the teachings should be easily accessible, and the teacher should be able to teach, otherwise they are either not a teacher, or they are bad one. If they are a bad teacher that can't teach, why exactly would you fill their empty spaces? At the very least, you should tell them to go learn their craft. Tell them to go learn their craft and come back and see them only when they do.

In addition to being trained to accept poor quality when it comes to spiritual teachings, we have also all been trained to blame ourselves when we do not understand some aspect of a teaching or a truth. Typically, what happens is that we will be presented with some poorly constructed spiritual verbiage. This presentation will explain hardly anything at all and will perhaps even add to our confusion and misunderstanding. Despite the obviously low quality of the spiritual teachings, we will accept the poor quality of the teachings and point the finger of blame at ourselves. Rather than giving the teachings an honest pedagogical assessment, rather than assessing the quality of the spiritual information on its own terms, rather than blaming a bad teacher for bad teaching and poor communicating skills, we look for fault within ourselves. If we cannot understand, we believe it is because we are too stupid, immature, or uneducated to understand. We may believe that just because they have written a book or advertised themselves as a spiritual teacher, then they must know more than we do. If we cannot understand, we believe it is because we cannot wrap our heads around the "deep" esoteric truths, that we are not "old souls", that we have "many lessons to learn", or it is all too deep and mysterious for us to understand. In short, we blame ourselves.

Why do we do this?

We do this because we have been conditioned to accept gnostic verbiage as divine wisdom and to blame ourselves for being stupid and unwise. We do this because we have been conditioned to believe that deep spirituality is ineffable, confusing, and complicated and so when we struggle with complicated, confusing, verbiage we do not question the verbiage, we question ourselves. In short, we have been conditioned to be sheep, thinking that we need the guidance of a shepherd; when the "shepherd" sucks, we have been trained to blame ourselves. In this way, we are spun around in impotent and ineffective circles.

This, I have to say, is a bit of a problem, and it is a problem because our self-blaming attitude interferes with our ability to understand the truths. The truth is the high/deep truths of creation are not that hard to wrap your head around, especially when presented by a competent teacher. The truth is even the profound nature of consciousness can be stated simply and transparently by a teacher if they a) understand what it is they are talking about, b) practice being a good teacher, and c) make an effort to communicate.

Therefore when you see complicated and confusing verbiage your first instinct should not be to turn critical attention on yourself, it should be to turn a critical light onto the teacher doing the teaching. *If a teacher cannot communicate in a grounded and effective manner it is their problem not yours.*

Of course, there is something to be said for "levels" of teaching. My own spiritual teaching for example moves from the introductory to the advanced. Introductory materials are, I feel, quite grounded and straightforward. I put a lot of effort into presenting the truths and communicating effectively so that everybody can understand what it is I am trying to say. I also put a lot of effort into the advanced materials, but if you jump right into the advanced materials, you could have trouble. Advanced materials assume familiarity with concepts and ideas taught at the introductory levels. If you do not have those concepts you will not understand, but not because you are stupid or incompetent, and not because I am necessarily a bad teacher. You will not understand simply because you do not have the foundation! Get the foundation and you will easily understand.

Still, as much as you do have to pay attention to "levels" of teaching, and as much as you have to be a good student and learn the foundations, you also have to be conscious of the fact that sometimes the teachings are simply poorly constructed, and the teacher is just incompetent. When that is the case, it is important to recognize their limitations and *not* blame yourself. If you are serious about spiritual progress, you are going to have to learn to discern between advanced teachings, incompetent teachers, and your own limitations. It is true that sometimes you have a lot to learn, but it is also true that sometimes teachers are just lousy teachers.

If you are presented with teachings that give you a headache while you are trying to figure them out, fly the red flag.

Maybe it is an advanced teaching that you do not have the foundation for, but maybe it is confused verbiage presented by an incompetent teacher. Learning to tell them apart can make the difference between consistent forward movement, or spinning your wheels and turning in circles.

Rocket Science (a.k.a. Rocket Speak)

Given the fact that a complicated teaching can either represent advanced teaching or poor pedagogy, and given that many of us have a propensity to blame ourselves rather than turn a critical eye onto the teacher and their teachings, how do you sort it all out and tell whether a teacher and their teachings are competent and worthwhile? There are a few things you can look at to help you sort it all out. First, be on the lookout for **Rocket Speak**[64] (a.k.a. periphrasis or, as I

---

[64] "'Rocket Speak'" is overly complex and contorted use of

also like to say, EPMO[65]). Rocket speak is unnecessarily complicated expression. Rocket speak is what you get when authors or speakers start to use a lot of really big words strung together in really complicated and linguistically distorted sentences. Rocket speak is common in the academy (i.e. when university professors and other intellectuals talk to themselves), but it also peaks out into the "normal" world as well. Rocket speak is a problem often, but it is a particular problem when it comes to spiritual teachings because spiritual teachings, which are ostensibly aimed at transforming the entire world, need to be open and accessible. Spiritual teachings are never about teaching just the "smart", "wise", "chosen", or "initiated". It is always about teaching to everyone regardless of anything. As soon as you get rocket speak you immediately cut off sections of the world's population from accessing the truth and that, by definition, makes for a bad spiritual teaching.

Of course, it is bad enough that we have to watch out for bad teachers, but rocket speak may indicate more than lack of training or poorly conceived pedagogy. The presence of rocket speak may actually indicate

---

language. Rocket speak is used to a) bolster the ego or b) hide the ignorance of a writer. Rocket speak is also be used, as in the case the esoteric verbiage of this planet, to c) confuse and misdirect. See http://www.thespiritwiki.com/Rocket_Speak/.

[65] EPMO stands for Egotistical, Polysyllabic, Multimetaphoric, Obfuscation. The term EPMO is a periphrastic way to refer to rocket speak.

deeper problems, like personal confusion, ego issues, and even a deliberate attempt to deceive. To put it as bluntly as possible, authors that use a lot of rocket speak may be

1. Confused and hiding that confusion behind EPMO.

2. Getting their ego needs met by using rocket speak to convey the impression they are smarter than, or superior to you.

3. Deliberately trying to confuse you to advance their special interests.

Let us look at each of these in turn.

Lack of Understanding: When it comes to personal confusion, here is the deal. Big words and complicated sentences obscure ignorance and confusion behind a brobdingnagian wall of periphrastic verbiage. When you do not understand what the writer or speaker is saying, it is difficult to sort it all out.[66] When it is difficult to sort out, then the writer can obscure their ignorance behind a wall of complicated verbiage. The

---

[66] You may even feel stupid for not understanding the big words he or she is using, especially if you had toxic socialization experiences. It happens often. Did you know what the words "brobdingnagian wall of periphrastic verbiage" mean when you first saw them, and if not, what did you feel when you realized you didn't understand what I was saying? Did you feel stupid? You shouldn't have. Those are big words and even I had to look them up in order to use them.

truth is, *you can obscure complete idiocy if you cover it over with a bunch of big words,* and this is certainly a problem. People who write to obscure their own lack of understanding obviously have nothing to contribute to yours.

Of course, at this point the question becomes, how do you identify when someone who is using big words does not really understand? That is easy: **ask questions**. You can tell a lot about a teacher's general level of expertise by how they respond to questions. For example, if you ask someone who does understand a question, they can usually explain it to in words you will understand. More importantly, if they cannot explain it they will usually admit that they do not know. They may sometimes show frustration at your question, and they may not like having to explain it, but they are going to be able to give you a satisfactory answer, even if that answer is an admission that they do not know.

By contrast, somebody who is covering over their own ignorance with EPMO will have a hard time with questions. It works like this. Typically, someone who does not truly understand will expend great effort to develop and control their script, prepare their monologue, and present their information. They do this to control your thinking and direct your consciousness so that you will not ask questions or engage in difficult dialog. Teachers that simply repeat lessons that they have been taught may be unable to answer your question. This is all fine and dandy, but carefully scripted productions fall apart if you ask the talent questions, and pull them away from their scripts. If they do not understand what it is they are teaching, if they do not have a solid foundation upon which to base their communication efforts, they flounder and struggle to answer, and not always in a subtle way. Sometimes they will get right pissed off and become aggressive and derisive towards you. If that happens, you know with absolute certainty you have triggered something stinky and foul.

Of course, angry and derisive outbursts are not common. It is not polite and it is too obvious a giveaway. Therefore, and typically, when individuals struggle with questions they do not understand they will simply not admit they are having difficulties. They do not admit because they cannot admit. Admitting that they cannot answer your question comes too close to admitting that they do not really know anything at all. It points them, and you, directly at their ignorance and they will be loath to point there. Thus, instead of admitting they do not know they will try to control and divert your attention away from the question. Individuals who divert attention from questions they cannot answer can utilize any number of strategies to divert you from the question you asked. They can divert you by pretending to answer your question while not really answering it at all; they can divert by answering a different question altogether; or, they can divert you by attacking you and trying to put you down.

If you are paying attention, it is usually easy to tell when somebody diverts your question by answering another one. It is also relatively easy to spot attacks. If, in response to a question you ask, a teacher starts trying to make you feel stupid or (worse) if they are trying to make others think you are stupid, you know they are trying to divert. Attacking you, or getting others to attack you, eliminates the need for them to answer your question directly and defends them against future inquiry. Pointing negative attention at you shuts you down and makes you look like and feel like the problem. Using people in the audience, they will ridicule you, disparage you, and get the audience to laugh. This attack effectively silences you at that moment, and even into the future. Are you really going to press your question, and are you ever going to stand up and ask another one, after being publically shamed and humiliated for doing so? This sort of thing ranks high on a scale of emotional and psychological abuse and is incredibly oppressive, especially when directed at children, adolescents, or young adults. Psychological damage may ensue.

The bottom line? Be on the lookout for rocket speak, and be especially attentive to attempts to suppress dialog and divert your attention. You can tell the difference between a bad teacher and a confused teacher by simply asking them a question and throwing them off script. Teachers who do not understand, teachers who are confused themselves, and teachers who are ungrounded have a very hard time with questions. *If you ask someone a question and they try to confuse the issue with complicated jargon or pedagogical diversions, fly the red flag.*

Ego Aggrandizement: As noted above, EPMO (i.e. complicated verbiage) is a red flag that certainly indicates bad teaching, but may also indicate lack of understanding and even confusion. You can flag a teacher's confusion by asking them questions. If they divert and/or attack, that is usually an indication they do not truly understand.

In addition to learning to deal with bad teachers, and teachers who are confused and using rocket speak to cover up their confusion; you also have to learn to deal with people with ego problems. People who use big words seem to be smarter than everybody else, and conveying that impression may be their primary intent. In other words, when you hear someone use many big words they may be trying to send you a message, and that message may be that they are better than you. If they are trying to send you that message, that is a bad thing, and not the truth! *If an individual is seeking attention and recognition of their superiority, it is usually because their ego has been damaged and their self-esteem has been destroyed.*[67] When an individual

---

[67] I should say here, being the center of attention is not always pathology. Some people actually love performing and being the center of attention, but not everybody that performs does so because they love it. Some do it simply to meet unmet ego or

has ego damage, using big words and complicated jargon helps elevate them in their own mind above those around them. In other words, using big words *feeds their damaged ego.* Therefore, someone using EPMO may be presenting as ego damaged.

Of course, having low self-esteem and/or ego damage does not immediately and automatically disqualify someone as a teacher. You can be messed up and still teach your pupils. At the same time, it does mean problems are more likely. Being ego-damaged can make it more difficult to express truth simply because people with low self-esteem prioritize their damaged self-esteem! That means that, among other things, *people with low self-esteem will say things to impress rather than say things to teach.* Obviously it is nice to get recognition for the great things you do, but when the priority is self-aggrandizement rather than self-less emancipation of others, the writer/teacher's goal may be to construct sentences that get people to go "wow is s/he ever smart" rather than "wow am I really God". In these cases, their ability to teach authentic spirituality may be compromised. Therefore, if your interest is in *moving forward,* do not settle. If you see a teacher using big words in an effort to inflate their own sense of self-importance, keep an eye out for self-esteem issues and ego damage.

---

childhood needs. If you are one of these people, if performing is not your passion, stop.

As you might guess from the above, it is relatively easy to identify an individual with ego problems. Typically, someone with ego problems soaks up attention and loves to be worshipped. You see this all the time on the late night talk shows on American television where some Hollywood actors literally bath in audience adulation. Of course, using worship and attention to assuage damaged ego and self-esteem does not disqualify you as one of Oscar's actors, but when it comes to spiritual teachers, it should raise some questions about the accuracy, authenticity, and motives of the teacher. The bottom line is, when egos are damaged and adulation becomes the goal, truth is shackled into the service of ego. If you see a teacher spewing EPMO, and if you suspect that EPMO is rooted in ego damage, fly the red flag.

Deliberate Deception: Confusion and ego-driven rocket speak are big problems in general, but an even bigger problem is the problem that comes when the people you trust to teach you aren't there to teach you at all but are instead there to deliberately deceive. In these cases, individuals use EPMO to obscure the deception. This may sound a bit paranoid to some, but it does happen. The truth is, authentic spirituality leads to authentic awakening, activation, and transformation and some people, in particular those who work for the System, would rather you not be empowered and transformed. The people who are not comfortable with your awakening and empowerment set out to deliberately mislead and confuse; and these days, what with the easy availability of YouTube and other accessible social media, their job is easier than ever. These days you do not have to turn very far at all to find someone spewing propaganda, ideology, and gibberish intentionally and specifically designed to daze and confuse. Of course, it is not always the case that people spewing propaganda, ideology, and gibberish are intentionally trying to deceive you. Sometimes they do it because they actually believe what they are saying, but whatever. Whether an individual does it on purpose or does it because they are a fool for the System doesn't really matter, because it is the same either way. When somebody is spewing ideology and propaganda at you then not a single thing they say is ever worth giving attention to!

As you saw above, identifying teachers who are confused or that have ego problems is fairly straightforward. You simply ask them questions, look for diversionary tactics, and pay attention to their attempts to elevate themselves. Unfortunately, it is harder to pin down the deliberate deceivers because their productions are often thoughtfully produced, carefully planned, tirelessly rehearsed, and professionally performed. Indeed, in the worst cases there can be entire teams involved in "handling" the "performer", the research, the production, and even the media attention. The only way to spot these deceivers is to either use your internal BS detector and discern up front that they aren't telling the truth (something you cannot do if your BS detector has been deactivated by bad advice and abuse) or watch carefully for the other red flags. If you see other red flags, like hierarchy, exclusion, hypocrisy, violence, ego, diversion and confusion, fly the red flag and ask some hard questions.[68] If you decide the person is a deceiver, run in the other direction.

Lack of Grounding in Reality

The presence of rocket speak definitely lowers the quality of teaching and is a powerful indicator that something funny is going on. It may not indicate deliberate malfeasance, but it certainly indicates the need to take a closer look. Another discernment red flag you need to pay attention to is reality, or rather awareness of reality. Authentic spiritual teachers, authentic priests and gurus, people who know what they are talking about, people who are enlightened and connected, know about reality, and by this I do not mean the Hollywood sitcom version of reality with the trouble free life-styles and the syncopated canned laughter. By reality, I mean the realities of this world, like the growing gap between rich and poor, the

---

[68] Interestingly enough, with the recent explosion of social media and the "direct connection" that so many performers now have to the masses, it has gotten a lot easier to spot red flags. It seems like every day now some peon of The System is, usually unwittingly, identifying themselves as a selfish, damaged, greedy, corrupt, ego-driven hypocrite. Either that or they are arrogantly flaunting their privilege and contemptuously shoving the "secret" sign of Baphomet up in your face. It is not always the sign of deliberate deception, but it sure is the sign of pre-empted spiritual development and damaged bodily ego.

prevalent child hunger, the greed, the violence, the war, the torture, the inequality, the political and economic madness, the looming ecological catastrophe, the sexual abuse, etc. By reality, I mean the nasty reality where governments on this Earth are more concerned to transfer trillions of dollars of public wealth into the private hands than help families and their children keep their lives and their homes intact. By reality, I mean the ugly reality of environmental degradation, political corruption, propaganda, and manipulation that exists all around you. You know... Reality! The bottom line is that spiritual teachers must have an awareness of reality.

Awareness of reality is a sine qua non of spiritual awareness and its absence is the single biggest red flag that there is.

If reality is not present in the information stream of a spiritual teacher it is a serious problem, and for two reasons. **Reason one:** lack of reality indicates lack of awareness, and lack of awareness equals, well, lack of Consciousness. Awareness, you see, *is* Consciousness, or at least one of the primary **Facets of Consciousness**.[69] Therefore Spiritual awakening necessarily brings you expanded awareness of the world around you. It is like sleeping at night and waking up in the morning. When

---

[69] A Facet of Consciousness is a term coined by Michael Sharp to represent the fundamental an indivisible facets of Consciousness. For more, see http://www.thespiritwiki.com/Facet_of_Consciousness/.

you are sleeping you are not aware of anything that is in your room. However, when you wake up you become aware of the room you are sleeping in. When you wake up you see the clothes on the floor, the clock on the nightstand, and the blankets on the bed. When you wake up you see the mess and there is simply no way around that.

The equation is simple. When you wake up your awareness expands and you see what is there. It is not rocket science and it is exactly the same with spiritual awakening. When you spiritually awaken, when you remove the Blindfold, you see the world and become more aware of reality. It does not necessarily happen all at once,[70] it does not mean it has to be pleasant, and it does not mean you automatically understand what you are suddenly seeing,[71] but it does mean you see what there is to see. *Expanded awareness of reality is the necessary result of spiritual awakening.* The more you are able to keep your eyes open, and the more of reality that you are able to see, the more enlightened and aware that you ultimately are. Awareness of reality is an essential correlate of spiritual awakening and a necessary outcome of expanded consciousness in body. Therefore, if reality is not present in a teacher's teachings, fly the red flag.

---

[70] Though powerful visions can result.

[71] There is a lot to take in after all, and what you see can be quite shocking.

The **second reason** that lack of reality is a red flag is because you cannot offer good spiritual advice to anybody if you do not know his or her reality. How can you teach somebody about the rarified connection of consciousness when you are not aware of their struggles with child abuse? How do you teach someone about chakra activation while their children are hungry and cold? How do you speak about disjuncture and alignment when you are ignoring domestic abuse? The truth is, you cannot. You cannot teach a person about God if you do not understand their reality. You cannot claim to speak for the truth when the words are devoid of a ground. Reality is critical. If you do not understand reality, then anything and everything you say will be devoid of said reality; and, if everything you say is devoid of reality, then all I can say is, *keep your delusions to yourself.* As for the rest of you, pay attention to this. *If a spiritual teacher does not take into account reality, do not listen to their advice.* If reality is absent, it is a sure sign that whatever advice they give will lack grounding and be devoid of sense.

A reasonable question at this point is how do you tell when someone is not grounded in reality? That is easy. **First,** look in the teachings. If there is no reality in their teachings then you know something might be up. I say something "might" be up here because sometimes people have a specific focus and that focus does not include regular discussion of reality, and that is OK. Just because an individual is not talking constantly about the horrors of the world does not mean

114

something is necessarily wrong. However, even though they are not talking about reality, they should still be aware it exists; so, if you do not see it in their teachings at all, ask a question or two to find out. What is their position on the growing gap between rich and poor, for example, and how does poverty affect a person's awakening efforts? Does violence in the home harm people's ability to connect? What is the impact of childhood trauma? Ask yourself the question, do they ignore these realities or do they consider and incorporate? Unless they grew up in an isolated community without technology, they should at least be aware of the relevance of reality to spiritual awakening and activation. *If they are not aware of reality, fly the red flag.*

The second thing you can do to tell if a teacher is grounded and present in reality is assess their commitment to reality/truth. Being aware of reality does not automatically make you a good source of truth. Many people see reality perfectly but either do not understand what it is they see or do not care that it is the way it is. Spiritual teachers can be totally aware of all the horrors of this planet yet not feel the need to consider these horrors against the foundations of their teachings. Many see the true and corrupt nature of the System, but accept the status quo anyway, or even end up "selling into it"[72], and/or working for it. They do this

---

[72] As Lady Gaga was once heard to say, presumably to justify her own choices.

not because they are evil but because they have been told, and they have come to believe, that the harsh realities of this world are irrelevant (or worse, necessary) to spirituality. You see this all the time! From Eastern stipulations to be "non-attached", to Western notions that everything happens for a reason[73], to New Age ideas that the "law of attraction" means you should just ignore reality so that it doesn't become more real,[74] to esoteric/masonic ideas that there is some kind of "balance" between "light and dark" that needs to be honored,[75] we are constantly advised to not be

---

[73] While it is true that many things do happen for a reason, sometimes the reason is not good, and sometimes the event is just random. If your child gets cancer and dies because of toxic metals in the environment, there is certainly a reason they're dead, but it isn't a good reason at all. Likewise if your child is playing on the street and is hit by a car, or abducted by a paedophile, there is a reason, but the reason is **unconnected** to God. If a plane falls out of the sky and kills you in your home, it is bad luck, bad maintenance, or bad flying, but it is certainly not divine planning.

[74] According to the Law of Attraction pundits, if you give something your attention you "give it energy" and bring it forward into reality. LOA pundits basically say that if you don't want something to come into reality, ignore it and pretend it is not there!??! All I can say to this is, if there is a thief in the store, a murderer in your midst, or a paedophile in your child's room and you pretend otherwise, bad things will happen and *you* will be just as much to blame. Ignorance and/or lack of concern are never acceptable excuses.

[75] This happens in Freemasonry, for example. It is clear that there is spiritual truth embedded in Freemasonry. However, it is also clear that the way they teach spiritual truth encourages acceptance of the status quo. The black and white checkerboard of their first degree tracing board is *visual ideology* that

concerned with the abuse in this world.[76]

I have to say, this sort of willful lack of concern is a problem in all cases because, as I say in *The Book of Light,* Consciousness is the root of all things. The world around you emanates from, and is created by, Consciousness. To be a little more direct, **Consciousness causes Reality**. That means the world is the way it is because Consciousness caused it. Since you are Consciousness, it makes absolutely no sense at all to disengage yourself from the realties or cares of this world as if they do not have anything to do with you. Disengaging in this fashion is like waking up in the morning to find your room on fire, and then sitting down and pretending it is not, or saying you want the fire, or even that God "planned" the fire and so therefore it is good. Any individual that is so uncommitted to reality that they are either unaware of the fire in the room, unconcerned about its implications and its consequences, or deluded into thinking God did it, is delusional and in need of serious professional attention. It is the same with a spiritual teacher. If a spiritual teacher does not display

---

encourages acceptance of the status quo. For more information on Freemasonry and ideology see http://www.thespiritwiki.com/Freemasonry/.

[76] A good overview of the lack of care and narcissism that has penetrated into the New Age movement is provided by Peter Marin, "The New Narcissism," Harper's 1975. Of course, the New Age movement is not the only spiritual tradition with alignment problems like this, but the article is instructive.

awareness of reality, if they encourage you to turn away from reality, or if they are totally unaware and unconcerned about said reality, they cannot claim to be awake and connected. It is not suggested that you buy into the fear, worry and anger that the System uses to control you. However, you must be aware of what is happening in the human reality. Remember, consciousness is Reality! *If reality is absent from the teachings, or is present only to be dismissed or ignored, fly, fly, fly the red flag!*

DISCERNMENT RED FLAGS – IDEOLOGY

At this point in our journey we have almost completed our tour of the red flags of spiritual discernment. So far, we have talked about identity issues, behavioral issues, and quality of teaching issues. Before closing this short treatise on discernment, I want to talk briefly about the final red flag, **Ideology**. *Ideology is an organized set of archetypes that provide untruthful justifications for the actions or inactions of individuals or groups.* [77] Ideologies essentially provide excuses for rotten behavior. For example, it used to be a widely accepted notion not so long ago that women were the "weaker" sex. Women were said to be overly emotional, weak-minded, and even childlike. Men on the other hand were the epitome of human evolution,

---

[77] For more, see http://www.thespiritwiki.com/Ideology/.

strong, rationale, and mature. These ideas represent **gender ideology**.[78] Gender ideology essentially provided (and still provides) men the excuse they needed to dominate, exploit, and exclude women from positions of power and authority. Exploitation and exclusion were natural and inevitable, or so the women were told. They happened because women were simply not cut out for men's work. They could not be allowed into the boy's club, could not be involved in any form of decision making, and in fact could have no authority either because "God" had set it up that way, or because evolution had determined women to be the "weaker" sex. Thus, it was "natural" and "divine" that women should be excluded from all positions of wealth, power, and privilege. Up until the suffragist movement at the turn of the twentieth century, they were. Before the suffragist movement came, women were considered so inferior to men they were not provided even the simple democratic right to vote, and thus were excluded from even minimal participation in civil society.[79] It was not that long ago that women had no formal power at all and nothing but their social clubs to go to, and that was OK because, as the men said, God/Nature made it that way. That is ideology. Ideology is all about justification

---

[78] For more, see http://www.thespiritwiki.com/Gender_Ideology

[79] Gender exploitation and ideology is still a feature of the world today. Even in so-called "advanced" industrial nations women still make only a fraction on the dollar of what men make, they are still primarily responsible for childhood and domestic duties, and they are still subjected to the oppressive memes of gender ideology.

and excuse for exclusion and exploitation. The gender ideology of the time justified and excused the domination, exploitation, and exclusion of women. It gave men an excuse, made them feel better about their callous exploitation and disregard of women, and it helped women accept the abuse and the exploitation by giving them a reason to capitulate.

Now, gender ideology is not the only ideology that we deal with in this world. There is also a **Racial Ideology.**[80] Racial ideology is ideology that justifies the exploitation of human beings based on the color of their skin. When white colonial Europeans ripped Africans from their home back in the "good 'ole days", they justified the slavery and abuse by telling themselves that the African's were not quite human; more like "mud babies"[81] or chimpanzees. Telling themselves this made it OK for them to exploit and abuse African's on the basis that they were barely human, merely animals. In the ideological realities of the old world, women were treated like children and Africans were treated as non-

---

[80] Fir more, see http://www.thespiritwiki.com/Race_Ideology

[81] There was actually a time when African's were called "mud babies". There is an infamous scene in Walt Disney's animated movie *Song of the South* where a black baby, a "tar baby" is created from a muddy slew. This scene is the most racist scene ever created and is probably the reason why Disney Corp. doesn't allow anybody to see that movie. They keep it locked away in their "vault" to hide their racist shame.

human.[82]

In addition to gender and race ideologies, there is also **Social Class Ideology.**[83] Social class ideology justifies exploitation and exclusion based on social class. Social class is your relative standing in the social hierarchies of this world. At the top, you have the rich while; at the bottom, you have the homeless. In between, we have the working and the middle. The rich live in their castles enjoying power and privilege while those below settle for less and are thankful for what they get. It does not matter that the rich got rich by exploiting the poor, stealing their land, harnessing their children, and forcing them into factories, it is justified as the way it should be.

Social class ideology is itself rooted in either **Scientific Ideology** or **Spiritual Ideology**. In science terms, hierarchy is justified because of the way evolution or nature works. It is the Darwinian order of things, the result of natural selection through natural competition. You cannot complain because exclusion, exploitation, and inequality are the natural way of things. You should

---

[82] Of course, the same thing happened to natives of America, natives of Espanola, natives of India, and so on. White people have a long, long history of exploiting and murdering anybody who did not have their pale, white, skin. This is just a basic reality of this planet. If you do not know this, it is because "they" do not teach it in school. They should, but they do not.

[83] http://www.thespiritwiki.com/Social_Class_Ideology/.

accept it because that is the way evolution works. Some people have the genetic chops, others do not. Some are the dominant "alphas",[84] other are not. It really just comes down to birth. According to social class ideology, some people are just born better and therefore "have what it takes". They got that "special spark", that bluish blood, the right talent, or the "strong" genes. As a result, they are smarter, wiser, stronger, and more capable than the peasants who gather below. It is their "special ability" and talent and not the number of ethical, moral, and personal compromises they have been willing to make, that has gotten them where they are. Because they are more worth/more evolved, they have a natural right to enrich themselves, take power, and get what they want.

Finally, we have **Spiritual Ideology**.[85] Spiritual ideologies justify exploitation, exclusion, hierarchy, and privilege by suggesting one group is spiritually superior over another. This ideology is expressed

---

[84] The notion of the "alpha male" is a good example of science used to justify inequality. Dominant capitalists are "alpha males," alpha males are part of the "natural order", so dominant capitalist are natural and inevitable. Recently however the scientist who coined the term alpha male to describe the behavior of male wolves has recanted, saying that there is no such thing as a "natural" alpha male. Now he says alpha behavior arises only in unnatural situations, as for example when male wolves are held in laboratory settings away from their natural environment and family! For the complete story see Mike Sosteric, "Ding Dong the Alpha Male Is Dead," The Socjourn (2012).

[85] http://www.thespiritwiki.com/Spiritual_Ideology/.

variously. Sometimes people say they are "chosen" by God, sometimes they claim to be members of some "great white brotherhood", some tell themselves they got better karma to work out and that is why they are lower, and so on. It is a reflection of the "divine hierarchies" in Heaven! It is the way God wants it; it is the way the universe works. We have God/King/CEOs at the top, angels/nobles/upper management a little lower, and the rest far below. In this case, the "chosen ones" are the ones who get the earthly rewards, get God's favor, and get into Heaven in the end. Those who are not "chosen" or are not members of the special club deserve whatever unhappiness, poverty, suffering, and despair they get. You should not complain; you should just accept it. It is God's great cosmic checkerboard after all.[86]

Identifying Spiritual Ideology

As noted above, ideology is all about justification and excuse. Based on this reading of ideology you would think it should be relatively easy to identify ideology in the words and teachings of the priests and gurus of this planet. Unfortunately, that is not true. Ideology is something we are indoctrinated into from a very early age. Almost from the time we can speak, system agents begin pouring ideology into our brain. This is a

---

[86] Peter Marin in an article entitled *The New Narcissism* provides a detailed overview of spiritual ideology as it emerged in the New Age movement in the early 1970s. See Marin, "The New Narcissism."

problem because when we absorb ideology at a very early age, our young and undeveloped brains cannot make a decision whether we agree with it or not, and it becomes a fundamental part of our psychic structures. As such, it can be very difficult for us to see, at least initially. This is not because spiritual ideology is technically hard to see. In fact, quite the opposite is true. Spiritual ideology is often obvious because of its patent absurdity. The problem is we do not see the absurdity because we have embedded it from birth. Because we are indoctrinated as children, it becomes an accepted part of our "normal" reality. As an accepted part of our normal reality, we do not even think about it, much less question it! Because we are indoctrinated as children, spiritual ideology is hidden in plain sight.

If you accept the existence of spiritual ideology, and you understand it can sometimes be difficult to see, the next question becomes, how do you increase your chances of seeing it? **Step one**, which we have already taken, is to the understand the general contours of ideology and spiritual ideology. As you now know, ideology provides ideas, archetypes, and statements that justify exploitation, domination, and exclusion. These shape spiritual ideology. If you see ideas, archetypes, and statements that justify and excuse, be on the alert for the presence of spiritual ideology.

Of course, there is more to identifying spiritual ideology than just looking for the obvious statements.

Once the blinders have been removed, it is easy to see the surface; however, the serpentine tendrils of spiritual ideology penetrate deep into the individual and collective consciousness of this planet, showing up in some surprising places.[87] Therefore, in addition to being aware of the general contours of spiritual ideology, **step two** is to be on the lookout for the red flags of spiritual ideology. These flags are the **"everything happens for a reason"** flag, the **fear factor** flag, and the **passivity flag.** These flags, while not the entire story by a long shot, nevertheless encapsulate the general tenor and tone of old world spiritual ideology. Let us look at each of these in turn starting with the idea that "everything happens for a good reason".

Everything Happens for a Good Reason

The first ideological red flag you should be on the lookout for is the "everything happens for a good reason" red flag. This flag should go up whenever you hear anybody try to tell you that all things, no matter how stupid, violent, or absurd they may be, happen for some kind of cosmic/divine/evolutionary reason. This flag should fly high whenever you hear someone trying

---

[87] For a look at one of the surprising places that spiritual ideology shows up, see Mike Sosteric, "A Sociology of Tarot," Canadian Journal of Sociology 39.3 (2014).

For a deeper look at the spiritual ideology of this planet than is possible here, see Michael Sharp, The Book of the Triumph of Spirit: Master Key (St Albert, Alberta: Lightning Path Press, Unpublished), Michael Sharp, The Book of the Triumph of Spirit: Halo/Sharp New Energy Archetypes, St. Albert.

to say that everything is a lesson from God, that all experiences no matter how painful make you stronger, or that it is all part of the natural order of things.

I am sure you have heard things like this before. Indeed, most people will be familiar with this red flag. You hear this sort of thing all the time, usually when someone asks "why all the suffering?" When people ask this question, the pseudo-teacher will done the mantle of spiritual authority and begin yapping about "God's plan", "life's lessons", "karmic justice", or some other ideological excuse for the status quo. The pseudo-teacher will tell you that "only God knows" or that "it's all in God's hands" or that "it's all part of God's lesson plan for you" or that "what doesn't kill you makes you stronger" and so on and so forth. They will tell you, essentially, to accept whatever "life" sends your way and be happy about it because experiences, even the very, very bad ones:

- Are good for you.
- Make you stronger.
- Teach you lessons.
- Evolve your soul.

Cancer of the prostate? It is not because of a bad diet or physical violence in your childhood, it is because God wants it that way. Grinding poverty and despair? It is not because of violent colonizing forces or greedy psychopath leaders, it is all part of God's plan! Beaten down by a corporate psychopath climbing the corporate ladder? It is not because of the nascent sociopathy of the corporate world, it is a part of the natural order! Survival of the fittest! Killed by a drunk driver on the street? It is not because of addictions and despair caused by a toxic System, it is because you "chose" that death or God wanted to bring you home.

We all heard these explanations before. Friends, family, the media, teachers, and other agents of consciousness reinforce them on a daily basis. However, for all their pervasive ubiquity, these ideas do not represent spiritual wisdom. On the contrary, they represent simple dissembling excuse for exploitation and exclusion. Bad things, and even good things, do not happen because God wants it that way or because they are lessons. You should not look for deeper meaning in the pain and suffering of this world. Bad things (and good things for that matter) always happen for a reason, and that reason is always linked to somebody's actions in the physical world.[88]

If you get cancer, it is not because of some directed divine event, it is because you did not take care of your

---

[88] Note that this does not mean that when things happen there isn't a spiritual cause. The operative word here is "linked". Because the universe unfolds from consciousness, the cause of anything is ultimately spiritual in nature. But, because we live in a physical universe, there is always a physical link. If you ignore the physical linkages then at best you aren't explaining the problem, and at worse you are abdicating all control and uselessly submitting before whatever forces, powers, and people do choose to act.

body, did not align with Consciousness, or were exposed to a carcinogen in your food, water, or air. If you get cancer, it is a mistake! There is no spiritual benefit to getting cancer at all and if you die from it, there is absolutely no good reason for that death. If you want to avoid cancer, do not buy into the ideology that justifies and excuses the deaths and protects those who poison our air; instead, take action! Do everything you can to take care of your body, isolate yourself from toxins, align yourself with Self, and stop the toxic flow.

If you were raped as a child or adult, it is not because you chose that experience or because that experience was part of your "lesson plan". That experience will not "make you stronger" or "make you what you are today". That experience will hurt you, damage you, undermine your trust in authority, disconnect you from Consciousness, damage your chakra system, break you,[89] and make it much harder for you to, connect with

---

[89] I'm not going to lie, the damage caused by violence of any type, much less the profound and toxic violence of childhood rape, is profound. It doesn't mean the damage is permanent. When handled correctly healing is possible. The truth is the human physical unit has remarkably sophisticated mechanisms and programs of self-healing. When these mechanisms are supported properly, even miracles become possible. The thing is though, in order to heal you first need to examine the wound and determine the cause of the damage. It is just common sense really. If you break your arm and the doctor doesn't take an x-ray or ask you how you broke it but instead says "it makes you stronger" or it was "God's plan for you", you're going to think the doctor is crazy. It should be the same when dealing with any form of assault, whether there is obvious physical damage or

others and with Consciousness. When an adult rapes a child (or anyone else for that matter) there is no benefit, there is no meaning, and most importantly, God is not standing behind it at all. When one person rapes another it is because the adult is emotionally and mentally ill, the parents are not there to protect the child, and society has turned away. There is no good reason for it; therefore, do not minimize the damage, and do not let it happen to you and yours.

If you're hit and killed by a drunk driver, if a corporation dumps toxic waste, if occupying soldiers kill your children, if rich bankers foreclose on your mortgage, a true spiritual teacher will never say, "oh well, that's life". A true spiritual teacher will point the finger at the true cause of the suffering, the actions of disconnected humans, not to judge and condemn the disconnected,[90] but to highlight the problems, identify disjuncture, and get you thinking about possible solutions. A true teacher will never say "it's God's will" or it's "nature's way". A true teacher will always stay grounded in reality, past *and* present. False teachers, teachers who work to justify, teachers who have

---

not. Examining the wound and determining the cause is the first step towards authentic healing.

[90] Judging and condemning a blindfolded and disconnected human would be exactly like getting mad at a sleepwalker for spilling some milk on the floor, which is to say, it is absurd. Once you realize this it is a lot easier let go and move on. As the avatar Jesus quite correctly said, forgive them for they know not what they do. Luke, 23:24.

embraced ideology and sold out to the System, will not. If you hear someone saying, "it is all part of the plan" or "it all happens for a reason" or "it is the natural order of things", especially when these words come as excuses and justification for pain, suffering, violence, and exploitation, fly the red flag. Listening to someone give you excuses will slow you down and turn you away from the work that needs to be done. It will also encourage misalignment, disjuncture, and consequent disconnection. If spiritual awakening and activation is your goal then this "everything happens for a reason" ideology is definitely something to avoid.

Before moving on to the next red flag of spiritual ideology allow me to say this. Just because I am criticizing the ideological notion that "everything happens for a reason" does not mean I do not believe that there aren't higher meanings that derive from spiritual action in the universe. I absolutely do believe that many things happen for spiritual, mystical, even God driven reasons. A chance encounter on the street that leads to positive benefit in your life may in fact not be a chance encounter at all; it might be an encounter encouraged by the divine activity of your guide network, for example. Of course, sometimes it might be a random event and have no higher meaning at all. Is it random or does it have meaning? That is something you have to decide for yourself, but keep the following key point in mind.

God may work in mysterious ways, but the ways of God

are supportive and love based, not punitive and pain based.

If you are suffering, it is because something <u>of this Earth</u> is making you suffer and not because God has a plan or karma is teaching you lessons. God, Consciousness, Spirit does not teach through suffering and hardship. Suffering and hardship happen that is for sure, and they happen for lots of different reasons, but they are not good for your body, they do not teach your soul lessons, and we, as a human species, should overcome them as quick as we can.

Fear Factor

In addition to the "it all happens for a good reason" red flag, another ideological red flag you want to be on the lookout for is what we might want to call the **fear factor**. The fear factor is the presence of fear inducing commentary and imagery in your information stream. This red flag is usually not that hard to spot because it is generally not very subtlety presented. It is also usually a very dramatic and unpleasant thing to experience. It is ugly, and when fear is present in the teachings it is a sure sign that something is wrong.

Now, this ugly fear factor thing is a lot more common than you might think. Obviously, Hollywood and the mainstream media use fear to scare people, but it is also present in the alternative media and on seemingly progressive websites. It is, indeed, peppered throughout the spiritual (and not so spiritual) discourse of this planet where you will hear many fear inducing statements like "the lizards are coming", "the rapture is upon us", "God is going to get you", "the end is nigh, so be very afraid", and so on. I would laugh and find humor in this if this fear-based material was not so psychically and spiritually damaging; unfortunately, it is very damaging. Fear shuts down your body's energy system. Fear constricts the flow and disconnects you from ground (root chakra) and crown (chakra). In other words, fear disconnects you from Source and makes you creatively impotent. It does this by putting your body into **Survival Mode.**[91] Survival mode is a mode of operation of your physical unit based not on the expansion of Consciousness but on its suppression! Survival mode is essentially an evolutionary program coded into the autonomic systems of your physical body. When your body is in survival mode, the higher cognitive functions of the physical brain are suppressed and control is devolved to the "lower" centers of the brain. When your body is in survival mode it essentially pushes Consciousness away and enters a more robotic/instinctual mode, where thoughts, actions, and behavior are based on survival programs stamped into the body by natural selection.

---

[91] For more see http://www.thespiritwiki.com/Survival_Mode. For a more detailed discussion of survival mode and the way it suppresses authentic spirituality and connection than I can get into here, see Sharp, Dossier of the Ascension: A Practical Guide to Chakra Activation and Kundalini Awakening. Also Sharp, The Book of the Triumph of Spirit: Master Key.

What puts your body into survival mode? Threat! When your body perceives a threat (real or just imagined) it automatically goes into survival mode. When your body is in survival mode it pushes higher Consciousness away and drops down into instinctual (i.e. programmed) response patterns. It does this essentially so that it can respond quickly to whatever threat it has perceived in the environment. Say, for example, that you find yourself face to face with a hungry tiger. In that situation, your physical unit is evolved/programmed to rely on instinctual response patterns, such as the so-called fight or flight response. Your body essentially says to itself, "I am in danger, I do not have time to think, I must act now", and it does. When your body enters survival mode, bodily energies/resources turn towards action, and control is devolved to lower brain centers. Adrenalin is released, blood is shifted to the extremities, and autonomic and survival programming kicks in.

Of course, when you are in danger, this is not a bad thing. *Survival mode has survival value* and it is a useful evolutionary feature of the physical unit. In the early stages of the evolution of the physical unit, when society had not evolved and where life was nasty, brutish, and short, the evolution of survival mode through the mechanism of natural selection increased the survivability of the Physical Unit. When your body is under threat, pre-empting higher consciousness and shifting into survival mode enhances survivability because it ensures rapid response, and that is a very good thing. However, when your body is not under real threat, survival mode is debilitating. Chronic release of adrenalin and cortisol lead to pathological changes in the body's physiology and neurochemistry. Chronic devolution of control to lower centers prevents Consciousness from descending into the vessel. Thus, any attempts to put your body into survival mode, by for example scaring you with tales of rapture, damnation, unemployment, terrorism, and attack, should be seen as an attempt to invoke your body's survival mode and prevent you from connecting to Consciousness.

Of course, a question that might arise now is, why would anybody want to put you into survival mode? The answer is, because a physical unit in survival mode is easy, easy to control. When your body enters survival mode, **Survival Mechanisms**[92] activate. Survival mechanisms are programs that, determine immediate behavioral and cognitive responses to threat. When a survival mechanism/program is activated, you act without thinking. If you see a lion running at you, survival programming takes over and tells your body to run. The automatic exit is a survival program that is activated when your body thinks it needs to flee to survive.

This automatic response pattern of your body when it

_____

[92] See http://www.thespiritwiki.com/Survival_Mechanisms/.

enters survival mode is exactly why you become so easy to control. When survival mode is activated, you are looking for a way to fight, escape, or comply[93] to avoid the threat. Knowledgeable actors can manipulate this mode in order to control your behavior. For example, if I am standing beside you and I open a cage and release a hungry lion, your body will enter survival mode. If I then yell at you and say "run that way", I am presenting you with a survival path. Once presented to you, you will very likely, and without thinking, run in the direction I tell you to. This is because a body in survival mode is programmed to make rapid survival choices, and there is nothing more rapid than following a directive. If you are in survival mode and I tell you to "run that way" or "the Jews are evil and taking your money", or "Russian Communists are after your freedom", or "radical Islamists are coming to kill your children", your body simply reacts. You do not wonder whether I am a trustworthy source; you do not evaluate the veracity of my statements; you simply follow my command.

There is a lot more to survival mechanisms, survival mode, and the exploitation of this mode to control than I can go into here. Suffice it to note, the fact that your body reacts without thinking is why system agents use

---

[93] For more, see
http://thespiritwiki.com/Fight,_Flee,_or_Comply. For a deeper discussion of the Fight, Flee, or Comply reflex, see Sharp, Dossier of the Ascension: A Practical Guide to Chakra Activation and Kundalini Awakening..

fear and threat to control. Fear and threat put your body into survival mode and make you easier to control. Without threat and fear, there is no control. If there is no hungry lion stalking you down, I can yell at you to run all I want, but you will not do it. As soon as you realized I was blowing hot air, I would no longer have easy control.

Of course, no system agent actually stands around opening lion cages to scare the peasants;[94] but there are other ways to scare you and put you in survival mode. If I threaten your livelihood, for example, by lowering the cost of oil and throwing your economy into chaos, if I say "radical Islamists are threatening your lives," if I can convince you that God is going to burn you alive and the only way to save yourself is to do exactly what I tell you to do, you'll do exactly what I tell you to. It is the same however you look at it.[95] If you are afraid, you

---

[94] At least not since the fall or Rome.

[95] Because of the nature of the Capitalist economic system, and in particular as a result of globalization and "austerity" measures increasingly imposed by governments, most people operate in a sort of chronic, low grade, survival mode. In this mode, which is intentionally activated by Capitalist economic policies, people tend to do what they are told without much question. Some people, particularly those trained in the elite socialization systems, like to call people in survival mode "sheeple".

As a side note, at this point you should be able to clearly see why calling people "sheeple", if this is a thing that you do, is such a moral and ethical injustice. Calling people sheeple diverts attention from fear campaigns designed to make people easier to control, and suggests that people are easy to control because of some internal (genetic, spiritual) weakness. Calling people

are easier to control. Remember this: *nothing trumps survival of the physical unit, not even Consciousness.*[96] Therefore, if you wish to retain control of your physical unit, be on the lookout for people pimping fear. True, they may be warning you about valid threats in the environment, and they may be offering valid solutions. On the other hand, they may be using fear and exploiting your body's survival mode in an attempt to possess your mind and control your body. Either way it is important to take a closer look. If the intent of the message stream is to notify you of problems, encourage your empowerment, and push you towards authentic solutions to problems in your (in our) world, fine. However if the point is to scare you, drop you into survival mode, and take control of your body and mind, fly the red flag and walk swiftly away.

"sheeple" (or whatever other names they use to degrade those they exploit), blames the victims for strategies the elites use to secure mass compliance.

[96] This is not quite true. It is possible for Consciousness to trump Survival Mode. This is typically accomplished when a wider definition of survival is being adopted, like for example survival of the family, or survival of a people. Parents, for example, regularly sacrifice themselves for their children and families. The father sacrifices his lungs in a coalmine so that his family can eat. The mother gives up a happy life for the slow misery of a bad relationship because she thinks it gives her kids a better chance. Similarly, political activists sometimes sacrifice themselves for the greater good of their society. We've all seen images of a monk lighting himself on fire in protest. In these cases Consciousness trumps survival, of the individual physical unit.

The Passivity Factor

The third and final ideological red flag I want to talk about in this booklet is the passivity factor. *The passivity factor is the idea, often couched in mystical bafflegab, that you are the passive and powerless victim of big cosmological forces, and therefore the best that you can hope for is passive acquiescence and obedience.* The message is always that these forces are bigger than you are and therefore there is nothing you need to do and nothing you can do but sit back, be passive, and accept. According to this ideological factor it does not matter what happens to you on this planet, just accept it because it is for some greater cosmological or theological good that you cannot understand. Everything is under control, everything is a lesson, and everything happens for a reason.

You can find these ideas expressed a lot by the so-called spiritual gurus of this world because it is a pervasive ideological corruption. In Catholic canon, for example, you are sheep, expected to passively accept whatever God sends you and to follow along with the commands of the shepherd. In New Age doctrine, it is the same. New Age authors encourage blind acceptance of the status quo by suggesting that to be spiritual means to "accept whatever is". One author says, "Whatever the present moment contains, accept it as if you had chosen it". Another repeats an ancient ideological aphorism when she says, "No experience is ever wasted because everything has meaning". Both statements encourage passive acceptance of "what is".

One says it explicitly while the other encourages passivity by implying that there is a deeper meaning behind all life events. Since all life events have meaning, you should accept the event as is, and look for the deeper meaning and positive aspects, even when the event is profoundly negative. This is of course classic "old energy"[97] theology. Larger powers are at work, bad things happen for a reason and you (silly little human that you are) can neither understand nor control them. Therefore, simply trust that "the powers" work for your own good and accept whatever comes your way.

Of course, this "old energy" ideology is all a bunch of nonsense, for two reasons. The first reason is that it is just not true. We are not passive sheep, we are not victims of powerful forces, God does not plan every little detail, and we are not kids in some cosmic schoolhouse. As I note in *The Book of Light,*[98] we are monadic intensifications in the glorious Fabric of Consciousness. We are sparks of divine Consciousness incarnated into a finely engineered physical unit. We are the Light and the Life. We have incarnated in the physical universe in order to express and create in

---

[97] Old energy is an LP term to describe violent, hierarchical, dominating, exclusionary, and elitist forms of energy. See http://www.thespiritwiki.com/Old_Energy/ and in particular Sharp, The Book of Life: Ascension and the Divine World Order.

[98] Sharp, The Book of Light: The Nature of God, the Structure of Consciousness, and the Universe within You.

alignment with, and in service to God Consciousness and Creation. Our body is the vehicle and tool for Consciousness and if we do not use our body, move our hands, shuffle our feet, take control, and make some changes, God, Consciousness, Soul, Spirit has no power at all. God works through the incarnated and connected monadic spark. As I said earlier, we are the Hand of God. If we just sit back and accept whatever comes our way we are going to put up with a lot of unnecessary oppression, suppression, exploitation, and abuse.

As noted above there are two reasons why the "passivity factory" is nonsense. One reason it is nonsense is because it is not true and it is not who we are. We are not passive sheeple, we in powerful sparks of monadic consciousness incarnated in a physical unit. **The second reason** it is nonsense is that it is a dangerous philosophy to hold. It is personally dangerous for sure. If you think that, "everything happens for a reason" or "God's got a plan" or "it all has a deeper meaning", you are going to be much less likely to pay attention and control your life. Indeed, you may even be actively discouraged from control. As Disney's *Frozen* advises, just "let it go". Put it on autopilot, cruise through life, and do not worry because everything is under control. To be sure the modern world isn't as dangerous as a jungle filled with lions, tigers, and bears, but dangers still exist and you have to be both aware of these dangers and proactive about their management. If you just go through life hoping and praying, you increase the likelihood of difficulty and tragedy.

Being passive in the face of life is personally dangerous that is for sure, but it is also globally dangerous. You would have to be blind not to see, but the world is in crisis. From economic catastrophe to ecological disaster to political violence, things are not getting any better. As noted in my *Rocket Scientists' Guide to Money and the Economy,*[99] the über rich have control of the economy, the government, and the banks, and they are acting in their own selfish interests. As a result, the people are suffering and the planet is dying. What we need now, what we have always needed, is the empowered action of the people of Earth rejecting power, privilege, inequality, greed, and corruption and building more divinely aligned alternatives. If "we the people" continue to sit back and accept, nothing is going to change. And if nothing changes, then as Lao Tzu said, you're going to end up where you are heading. The bottom line, if we do not stand up, if we do not move, if we do not align with the Light, if we do not work towards the highest good, nothing changes.

Which of course, may be the intent.

People who encourage you to sit back and let go, people who tell you that there's a greater power at work, people who say sit back and "attract" rather than

---

[99] Sharp, The Rocket Scientists' Guide to Money and the Economy: Accumulation and Debt.

get out and transform, people who say it all happens for a reason so passively accept may be intentionally creating impotence in order to enhance and protect their own power and privilege. Standing back and letting things passively happen benefits the powerful and privileged status quo. Anybody that tells you to just sit back and passively accept is, wittingly or unwittingly, working for said status quo, period. If you want my advice, do not fall for the passivity factor. Pay attention to events and take control of your life. If somebody is telling you to be passive, lie back, close your eyes, do not worry, let it go, let it happen, etc., fly the red flag! Stand up, embrace your light, and return to full power.

That is all I have to say about the topic of spiritual ideology here. Before closing this book, I just want to say that the topic of spiritual ideology is a big topic and an important one for any intermediate and advanced practice of spirituality and spiritual discernment. Unfortunately, there is limited space in this short monograph to deal with it. If you want the extended treatment, see my *Book of the Triumph of Spirit* series.[100] In that series I expose the spiritual ideology of this planet in detail, and provide alternative ideas that you can use to replace spiritual ideology that creates impotence with ideas and archetypes that awaken, activate, and transform.

---

[100] http://press.thelightningpath.com/triumph-of-spirit/

Conclusion

This brings to an end this *Rocket Scientists' Guide to Discernment*. In this book, we have looked at a few discernment red flags that you can use to help you decide whether information streams you follow are worth staying connected with, or whether you should dump and move on. I hope that at this point you are on solid ground *vis a vis* your ability to winnow the wheat from the chaff. If not, reset your intent (i.e. "I want the truth and nothing but, no compromise, no strings attached") and re-read the book. Take some notes, use yellow sticky note, underline, and do whatever it takes to ensure that you are cognizant of, and looking out for, the discernment red flags.

Before closing up I would like to mention one final red flag and that is the red flag of authority. If there is any single lesson you should take from this book it is this: never take anything on authority. Just because somebody has a degree, has written a book, claims to be a world teacher, wears the right robes, sits on the right chair, speaks the right words, has the right ring, gives the right handshake, displays the right symbols, has been to the right shaman, or has taken the right entheogenic substance does not mean they know diddlysquat about Consciousness, the Body, and Creation. In fact, it is possibly exactly the opposite. In an age where money can buy anything including followers, any one with money can build a club and buy their way into it. The real teachers, the authentic teachers, the powerful teachers, do not "buy in", "sell in", or sell out. Real world teachers, authentic teachers, whether these teachers are singers, painters, writers, or whatever, never make it about their ego, their prosperity, their privilege, or their power. Real teachers always make it about you, your Divinity, your Light, and your power. In short, real spiritual teachers, authentic teachers, put the authority in your hands by bringing you back to the divinity that is inside you. If you are steered in any other direction than that, fly the red flag and run quickly away.

I am serious here! The time for being followers, peons, and docile spiritual slaves is over. The time for putting up and shutting up is done. Remember, you are the ultimate creative authority over your life. So, wake up, stand up, and march. It is the only way to save the planet. It is the only way you are ever going to get reconnected to Consciousness. It is the only way to make it back home.

March 15, 2017

About the Author

Michael Sharp is a Sociologist with a specialization in psychology, religion, occult studies, social inequality, scholarly communication, and critical theory. After a dramatic crown chakra opening caused him to question the materialist foundation of modern science, he began exploring the spiritual and mystical side of life. Recognizing early the presence of elitism and patriarchy in the world's religious and "secret" traditions, he began creating a new, open system of mysticism free of the opportunistic bias in "old energy" systems. The Lightning Path is the culmination of his research and work. Visit Michael at http://www.michaelsharp.org/.

About the Lightning Path

The Lightning Path™ is an intellectual, emotional, psychological, and spiritual system of awakening and activation (a "mystery school" if you like, but without all the useless mystery) designed to help you get off the sinking ship of the old world and make "the shift" into an awakened, activated, and ascended state of existence. It is sophisticated, powerful, logical, grounded, rational, intellectually and metaphorically rigorous, politically sophisticated, empirically verifiable, authentic, effective, and accessible to everyone regardless of race, class, or gender. For more visit http://www.thelightningpath.com/.

Other Books in the Rocket Science™ (RSG) Series

RSG to Money and the Economy

- Print ISBN 978-1-897455-12-1
- eBook ISBN 978-1-897455-18-0

RSG to Spiritual Discernment

- Print ISBN 978-1-897455-16-6
- eBook ISBN 978-1-897455-17-3

RSG to Authentic Spirituality

- Print ISBN 978-1-897455-12-8
- eBook ISBN 978-1-897455-13-5

For more books by Michael Sharp, visit http://press.thelightningpath.com/

References

Ellens, J. Harold. *The Destructive Power of Religion: Violence in Judaism, Christianity, and Islam*

Ed. Ellens, J. Harold. Vol. 1. 4 vols. Westport, CT: Praegar, 2001.

Marin, Peter. "The New Narcissism." *Harper's* 1975: 45-56.

Sharp, Michael. *The Book of Life: Ascension and the Divine World Order*. St. Albert, AB: Lightning Path Press/Avatar Publications, 2003.

---. *The Book of Light: The Nature of God, the Structure of Consciousness, and the Universe within You*. Vol. one -air. 4 vols. St. Albert, Alberta: Lightning Path Press, 2006.

---. *The Book of the Triumph of Spirit: Halo/Sharp New Energy Archetypes*. St. Albert.

---. *The Book of the Triumph of Spirit: Master Key*. St Albert, Alberta: Lightning Path Press, Unpublished.

---. *Dossier of the Ascension: A Practical Guide to Chakra Activation and Kundalini Awakening*. Lightning Path Press, 2003.

---. *Lightning Path Workbook One - Introduction to Authentic Spirituality*. Lightning Path Workbook Series. Vol. 1. St. Albert, Alberta: Lightning Path Press, 2016.

---. *Lightning Path Workbook Three - Foundations*. Lightning Path Workbook Series. Ed. Sharp, Michael. Vol. 3. St. Albert, Alberta: Lightning Path Press, 2017.

---. *Lightning Path Workbook Two - Introduction to the Lightning Path*. Lightning Path Workbook Series, St. Albert, Alberta.

---. *The Rocket Scientists' Guide to Authentic*

Spirituality. St. Albert, Alberta: Lightning Path
 Press, 2010.

---. *The Rocket Scientists' Guide to Money and the
 Economy: Accumulation and Debt.* St Albert,
 Alberta: Lightning Path Press., 2016.

Sosteric, Mike. "Ding Dong the Alpha Male Is Dead."
 The Socjourn (2012).

---. "A Sociology of Tarot." *Canadian Journal of
 Sociology* 39 3 (2014).

Index